To BECKY, LYNN and MARY LOU
with whom I've shared so much,
from whom I've learned so much.

Contents

Preface

For over twenty years I have served in Bangladesh first as a nurse and more recently as the missionary director of our Literature Production and Distribution Center. During this time I have been impressed with the need for better communication and over-all better interpersonal relationships between the married and non-married members of the missionary community. This is no less true in non-mission circles.

Then, on two occasions I have been asked to lecture on the subject at the Candidate Classes of my mission, The Association of Baptists for World Evangelism (ABWE). The content of *By Ones and By Twos* stems from these lectures. The real life illustrations come from experiences—positive and negative.

Introduction

Focus On The Frustration

Wimbledon—Forest Hills—the very names ring with excitement and drama!

As opponents face each other across the net, one thought is uppermost in both minds: to play well; to win.

Sometimes the game is a singles match. Tennis, however, is just as frequently played by doubles: two partners competing with another two players. Singles or doubles, the court, the equipment, the rules are the same and the goal for each opponent is to win the prize.

Tennis as we know it did not originate until the 1400's. However, the game has its roots in a type of handball played in ancient Greece and in Rome. So it could be that Paul had that game in mind as well as track and boxing when he admonished the followers of Christ to "Press toward the mark," "Fight the good fight," and "Run the race."

In the game of life and Christian service, it would appear that some Christians have forgotten the unified purpose and have become caught up with the status of the "players," dividing them into two categories, the married couples and the singles (usually the "single girls"—be they 22 or 62 years old).

I had never run into the term "single missionary" until I became one. In the business and professional world a person is a secretary, a waitress, a nurse; not a *"single"* secretary, waitress or nurse. I don't know where or when the label "single" was affixed to an unmarried missionary woman. I was introduced to the term in missionary candidate school.

My candidate class was held in a beautiful mission home in Germantown, Pennsylvania. This was in the years before the Memorial Christian Hospital to be built in Bangladesh was even off the blueprints; but already people were sending supplies to the mission office: empty medicine bottles, rolled bandages, old eye glasses, used clothing, etc. (I remember we had a fashion show one evening and sent our colleagues into hysterics contemplating the graceful Indian women for whom the odd assortment of garments were intended, wearing some of the getups).

Candidate school included work assignments for each of us. The medically oriented candidates were assigned a basement area where we were to sort out the useful items for sending for the hospital.

One afternoon I was working in a corner that blocked the ping-pong table. Naturally everyone wanted that section cleared away first. But there was a heavy box which I could not lift. So, going to the stairway, I called to the first person I saw, who happened to be a young married man, "Would you come and help me, please?"

I'll always remember his answer, "I might have known. They *told* me I would be helping 'single girls' all the time and already it's started."

Now, my marital status had nothing to do with the fact that I had sought his help. Had I had five husbands, I still could not have lifted that heavy box!

Later, during those four weeks of candidate school, someone broke a rule. I don't remember what the infraction was, but immediately the single women were blamed for whatever had happened. *Fine,* I thought. In some places they tease bald men, some places it's red heads; here they pick on the unmarried people.

It had not dawned on me that my being a single missionary conjured up in people's minds a whole complexity of problems; a whole list of potential difficulties for myself and those who would have to work with me.

This stereotyping has continued in missionary circles even with singles carving an important place for themselves in Western society.

Ten years after my class, a group of 43 candidates gathered for their mission orientation. At the close of the school, after a month of warm fellowship the couples expressed how much they had enjoyed being with eight unmarried women candidates. Some freely admitted that they had heard things which had predisposed them to think this would not be so; that there would be trouble. They had been pleasantly surprised.

While I was on my first deputation tour, many times people remarked about how difficult it would be to get to the mission field due to my being single. I found that was just not so.

From time to time I've received questionnaries concerning the general attitude of churches toward the single missionary. Included were such items as:

1. Do you feel that travel for the single missionary is More difficult _____ less _____ More expensive _____ less _____ same as for marrieds _____?
2. Do you feel that lodging for the single missionary is More available in homes _____ less available _____ same as for marrieds _____?
3. Should the single lady be permitted to speak in Sunday A.M. service? Is she invited to do so often _____ seldom _____ same as other missionaries _____?
4. How does the attitude of the local church appear to compare between the single lady missionary and a couple? Is she more acceptable _____ same _____ less acceptable _____?
5. Are the opportunities to speak to groups other than the Sunday A.M. service unlimited _____ somewhat limited _____ very limited _____?
6. Do you feel that personal finances per individual missionary is obtained more easily _____ less easily _____ same as for couple _____?
7. Do you find both prayer and financial support more difficult to obtain _____ less difficult _____ same as for couple _____?

One questionnaire covered eleven topics complete with subheadings. In most instances the only reasonable answer is "Same as for a married woman." Traveling, housing, speaking in churches: these can all pose problems, perhaps more so for some than others. But most likely that "some" consists of married women and their husbands as well as unmarried women missionaries.

It's unfortunate that mission boards and other sending agencies perpetuate and accentuate this *difference,* rather than majoring on integrating all their personnel, married and single. One mission sent out a list headed, "Occupations for Single Lady Missionaries." The jobs listed were:

Nursing	Lab Technology	Physiotherapy
Journalism	Art/Layout	Bookeeping

Actually, any one of these jobs could be performed by any qualified missionary. So the point of emphasizing "single lady missionary" escaped me.

Even the use of the words "single" and "unmarried" interchangably can create confusion. For example, I once received what I took to be a very great compliment. It was this: "She has done more in this area than any other single person." Wow! I was impressed. I thought that meant that I had accomplished more in the particular area than anybody else had! I learned that the speaker meant more than any *unmarried* person. (Since to my certain knowledge no unmarried person had ever tackled that particular job, the compliment lost its imput). The issue was not my receiving or not receiving a compliment; but if I were to receive it, why not let it be for my achievement, married or not.

It's true that we all take with us as we start out on a career or calling, certain preconceived ideas and fixed expectations. For example:

A new missionary family had arrived in Chittagong, Bangladesh, the city where I work. I invited the young wife over to my house and soon we were chatting and laughing and having a nice time over coffee. We talked about her family back in the States, the experiences on the trip to Bangladesh, and the house that the family would soon be moving into. As she was leaving, she remarked, "I didn't know—I never expected—that I'd be able to sit and talk like this with a single girl."

I recall pondering, *Why would she suppose that she wouldn't be able to talk with me?* At the same time I felt good about the rapport we had obviously established.

What is more conducive to on-going effective Christian service than rapport and harmony among fellow workers?

What is more destructive than poor interpersonal relationships?

One area of life where harmony can become discord is in the relationship between unmarried workers and their married co-workers. In the missionary world this deserves special consideration because:

Statistics show that 39% of the overseas missionary force is men. Since the majority of those are married, let us assume that 38% of the remaining 61% are their wives. This leaves a sizeable 23% of the total missionary force women who, by choice or circumstances, are not married.

An executive of my mission, visiting the field, discussed proposed changes in the Candidate Orientation Program. He suggested the holding of separate sessions for the married and the non-married so that each would be discussing areas which pertained to them. There is, of course, a need for a limited number of such segregated sessions. However, the greater need would seem to be our focus on the similarities of our task, the oneness as we serve the Lord together wherever He has called us.

Separating the group by marital status seems to emphasize differences rather than promote unity and harmony. We who are involved in Christian service hold many things in common. We are all persons; we are striving to carry out God's plan and purpose for our lives. We have similar hopes, aspirations and goals. Thus sessions stressing points of common interest and sharing ideas on how these can be implemented, would be infinitely more productive than those which perpetuate a destructive dichotomy among missionary personnel. And who is to say whether today's single missionary will be one of tomorrow's marrieds. Or today's wife, tomorrow's widow?

How much better to try to bridge gaps: between younger and older; between men and women; between the married and the unmarried.

But how to do this? It's not enough to recognize that there is built-in potential for problems in the interpersonal relationships and to theorize about how to avoid or handle such problems when they arise.

The following chapters offer some principles which, I trust, if put into practice, can lead to commendable harmony in living and working together.

In suggesting these principles, I realize that people tend to react negatively to being told what to do and not to do. Generally we prefer being given a list of options and negotiable points, considering each then deciding on the issue. Such, apparently, was not always so.

I have in my library an archaic, out-of-print book with the one syllable title, *DON'T*. The equally off-putting subtitle is, "Mistakes and improprieties more or less prevalent in conduct and speech." For 96 pages it gives line upon line of, "Don't do this; don't do that," with an occasional more positive, "Don't neglect to—." Here are a couple of admonitions:

"Don't wear your hat cocked over your eyes, or thrust back upon the head. The one is rowdyish, the other rustic"

"Don't use the word 'sick' except when nausea is meant: say 'ill' or 'unwell' or 'indisposed'."

Enough of that, except to mention that, for clarity in understanding,

I will resort to presenting some points through do's and don'ts.

Most of my real-life illustrations and examples are from Bangladesh because that is the part of the world with which I'm most familiar.

I want to say to the glory of God and the praise of our missionary community that we have had a minimum of conflict in this singles/doubles realm.

An example of our fine interpersonal relationships is this recommendation which was unanimously adopted by our Field Council. After 16 years of close association with single co-workers, Dr. Donn Ketcham wrote,

> Dismal reports and dire prophecies from other areas to the contrary notwithstanding:
> Whereas the single ladies on this field have proven to be the most congenial colleagues, and
> Whereas the single ladies on this field have continued to make contributions that are among the most important of all contributions made by our team,
> The married members of this Field Council pass this resolution whereby we express to them our deep love and appreciation and our thanks to God for the honor of serving by their side.

Gratifying as such an affirmation is, in even good situations there is always room for improvement.

There are areas where there is need for clearer understanding; there are harmful breakdowns in interpersonal communication; there needs to be mutual sensitivity as to remarks and situations which cause friction.

As we look into these situations, we will switch back and forth from singles to doubles; from unmarrieds to marrieds in order to relate to each most fully. Ready?

Chapter One

The Know-it-all Colleague

A Christian national remarked, "I wish that once—*just once*—when I ask a question, a missionary would admit, 'I don't know.' "

What did he mean? Where did such thinking stem from?

Just this: As a group, missionaries tend to be achievers. Their education, specialized training and a degree of expertise can often come across to others as a form of omniscience. And this insightful national could see through it.

Of course, in this age of specialization and ever-increasing knowledge, no one can ever possibly "know it all." We must be careful, even those who are genuinely well-informed, not to give the appearance of being a walking encyclopedia before either our national or missionary colleagues.

To the *unmarried:* It may be that for one reason or another, you have had more opportunities for formal education and have earned more degrees than your married missionary sister has. Even so, don't assume that just because you have a string of letters after your name, you are the final authority on any subject. Perhaps the other woman didn't graduate from college; but she might have had more practical experience. Perhaps in a job situation, in counseling, in rearing her own children, in being a pastor's wife she has gained valuable wisdom and knowledge. Listen to her and don't lightly discount her suggestions.

Now to the *married* side: Possibly most of your time is spent in being a good homemaker. Even so, don't let that cause you to assume tha you are the epitome in that field. Housekeeping, home decorating, cooking are all skills which can be learned. As in every other sphere, some people have a flair for certain aspects which makes them out-standing where others may be mediocre. The flair can, however, apply to any woman—married or otherwise.

I think of a woman named Kathy Kendall. The first time I spoke on this singles/doubles topic, Kathy provided an illustration. I recalled that at my own Candidate Class she had been conscripted to bake the cinnamon coffee cake and featherlight dinner rolls for which she was famous. The next time I saw Kathy was in her home in the outskirts of Manila where she was acting Dean of Women at a Bible School. Her living quarters there, though small, were tastefully arranged; in every sense of the word hers was a home, a place where students could feel welcome and free to sit down, talk over their concerns, and relax from the pressures outside. Then—she up and got married! I don't know if that proves my point or disproves it! Since her marriage I've had the pleasure of being entertained in their home and have found her the same gracious hostess, the same excellent cook in her pleasant surroundings.

It's a fact that sometimes an unmarried woman can give good tips to the married.

The same appears to be true in regard to caring for children. The biological fact of having given birth does not, in itself, necessarily make a woman a good mother. Think of Amy Carmichael, of Gladys Aylward (the "Small Woman"): women whose names have gone down in history as having been wonderful mothers, although they never had a child of their own. Natural parenthood does not guarantee a built-in knowledge of children's needs and how to meet them.

A phrase sometimes thoughtlessly tossed out by married people and which can cause pain to the unmarried is: *"You* wouldn't know any-thing about this; you don't have any children." The one being spoken to may in fact have a world of experience with children, or—which is more painful—the possibility of not having children of her own may be the hardest trial of not being married. To have this rubbed in by careless words is not necessary. Most little girls play with dolls; most young women assume they will marry and have children. When it ap-pears that those dreams will not be realized, there is generally enough disppointment without reminders through either unwitting or inten-tional remarks from married colleagues.

So, parents, try to accept gracefully suggestions concerning your children. This is especially important if you have single people teaching your children. A few years ago I overheard a conversation following a challenge of the needs of a certain South American country. One of the women entering into the discussion was the mother of two small children. Unfortunately she had not learned her English well. We were discussing why it was that a particular field had so few missionary applicants. This young woman in a heated voice asked, "Why hasn't more went?" Later she explained one reason why she had chosen the Mission Board under which they planned to serve:

> "In this Mission I'll be allowed to teach my own children, and not have to turn them over to some old maid teacher who could never have children of her own."

Apart from anything else, such a speech is destructive of good relationships. Be careful about such a know-it-all attitude.

There may be times when, married or not, you really do know more about the subject under discussion than others present. We would hope, then, that your associates will be wise enough and mature enough to take your knowledge and expertise into account. But usually, unless they ask for your contribution, it is wise to keep your know-how to yourself. In writing about our relationship with God, the Psalmist advises, "Be still." That's also good counsel for human relationships.

We are all familiar with individuals who seem to have to hear themselves talk. No matter what the topic, they have something to say. They butt into conversations. They deflate a person by following his story with, "Oh, *that's* nothing. You should hear what happened to me . . ." They have had every illness (except of course emotional illness—all their friends have had that). They ruin conversation by monopolizing it. Wise was the man who wrote,

> It's better to keep your mouth shut
> And have people think you are ignorant,
> Than to open it—and remove all doubt.

Remember God's rebuke to Peter on the Mount of Transfiguration? Impulsive Peter could not just bask in the glory and awe of the experience. He *had* to say something. What he blurted out was a real gem. "It is good for us to be here." Sounds as if he was attending a tea party. God cut him off short, *"While he thus spoke . . ."* God spoke, *"This is my beloved Son: hear Him."* Our God is too polite to be vulgar, but a loose translation of His words would come out something like, "Shut up, Peter, and listen, for once."

Often our words spoil our 'usefulness. We go to comfort someone in trouble or bereavement. Instead of just being there, just sitting perhaps with an arm around our friend, we *have* to talk. And such words as we say! "I understand," "I know all about it," when, unless we have been through an identical experience, we cannot possibly understand the pain our friend is feeling. How much better just to be there not speaking, not doing—just being. When there is nothing appropriate to say, try saying nothing.

New missionaries especially have to guard against knowing-it-all and saying-it-all. And here I speak from bitter experience. I was young when I arrived in Chittagong, a new R.N. with two and a half additional years in a Christian College that earned me a B.S. I had grown up in a home where missionaries and heads of mission boards were constant visitors. The question between my older brother and me when we moved to a new house was, "Do you want the big bedroom you have to give up to the missionaries or the little one you can keep to yourself?" Attending missionary conferences, especially the king of the conferences—People's Church in Toronto, Canada—had been a highlight of my childhood years. I still recall the curio tables with the scorpions in bottles, and booklets written in exotic languages. I had been teaching children since I was a child of eight myself. I had sung and "said missionary pieces" in churches and conferences throughout the United States and Canada. One especially poignant piece, whose author is unknown will haunt me as long as I live. It was particularly appropriate during the years my father was the Canadian Secretary of The Mission to Lepers:

> Ten lepers stood at the break of day
> At the roadside rim,
> For they heard men say
> That the dear Lord Christ would pass that way,
> Pass by the side of the road.

In many more stanzas it depicted the plight of those suffering from leprosy prior to the advent of the sulfones, and the inventions of Leprologist, Dr. Paul Brand.

Oh yes, I "knew all about being a missionary." I knew what I would be doing when I arrived and what everyone else ought to be doing. And what's more, I said it! Vociferously. I scorned the practice of having household help. I would do all my cooking and cleaning myself, thank you. I objected to the rule of a solid year of language study without being allowed an outside ministry. I criticized the program being offered to the missionary children for their spiritual growth.

It took a long time—too long—to bring me down from my elevated idea that I had all the answers. My colleagues were so loving and patient. They helped me understand the whys behind the practices and policies. Together we worked out programs which were mutually beneficial. But many times since those days I have wished that I had just kept quiet.

For some of us this is a problem we will have to work on all our lives. Recently my housemate Lynn Silvernale and I returned from an evening meeting to be greeted by our neighbors saying, "You had a visitor from the hospital . . ."

Without waiting to hear the details, I started in with, "Why did they come tonight? They wrote that they were coming tomorrow. Why can't people do what they say they are going to do?"

I noticed that Lynn, was trying to say something, but I barged ahead, "Where will they sleep? We don't have anything ready. Why didn't they let us know?" Suddenly the next door neighbor enlightened me that the person who had come had nothing to do with the ones I was talking about. Later I asked Lynn why she hadn't told me I had made a mistake about the people.

She replied, "I didn't think it was worth it. You already had your mind made up."

That was another one of the many times when I would have done well to have remembered the old Chinese proverb, "Closed mouths gather no feet."

By contrast, four years after my arrival in Bangladesh, a couple with pastoral experience in the United States came to join our team. At their first business meeting a point of church polity as it relates to a cross-cultural situation arose. The new man was asked his opinion. He replied, "I think we'll just listen this time." What a wise man.

Please don't misunderstand. I am not saying that new missionaries should be "seen but not heard." Any organization which does not allow for new ideas, new patterns of learning, new methods of outreach, will stagnate. Any group which operates on the principle "we've always done it this way," is doomed. Sometimes the greenest recruit fresh into the country will bring insights hidden from the rest. Sometimes the newcomer will have been exposed to approaches that have worked elsewhere and might work well in his new field. New thoughts, new ideas, new people are welcome. It is the attitude, the garb in which all this newness is clothed that is important. A humble attitude that suggests, not insists; a concern that ask, "Do you know about . . .; Have you read . . .?": these will produce much better results than my "bull in the china shop" approach. It all goes back to the opening words in this chapter, being willing to admit, "I don't know," rather than having to know-it-all.

Chapter Two

Adopting a Family Attitude

A beautiful verse with deep meaning for those far from home is Psalm 68:6, *"He setteth the solitary in families."*

Missionaries live in two worlds. For two, three or four years at a stretch their home is in a foreign culture. Yes, they try by letters, pictures, tapes to keep up with their families back in their home countries; but life goes on whether or not they are there. New nieces and nephews are born, star in school productions, graduate, marry. The missionary returns to his own family and often feels like an extra at a party.

Gradually, however, the missionary is weaned away from home and finds a new "home" with those among whom he has come to work.

On the mission field one may live in close contact with a wide range of people: Long time missionaries, new recruits and the children of each of these. All speak the same language—both literally and figuratively. Everyone lives through the same frustrations, weathers the same crises and, it is to be hoped, grows to be long-suffering towards each others' foibles. This sense of belonging is never as clearly seen as when two people from the same mission field meet while on furlough. I have had this happen to me a number of times: a tall teenager comes bounding across his college campus with an unembarrassed, "Oh, Aunt Jeannie!" as we talk our heads off getting caught up on news from "home."

I had been on furlough about eight months when an assignment from the mission office brought six or so of us from the same field together. One young wife on her first furlough rushed up and hugged me. Then earnestly she said, "A year ago, if anyone had told me I'd be happier to see you than my own sisters, I would have said they were crazy. But it's true. We each know what the other one means. We can talk together." And we did!

Another furloughee expressed a common feeling, "I love my family here at home, but when I really need help in thinking out decisions, I feel I have to share the problem with someone from the field."

"He setteth the solitary in families" You may be a prospective missionary who doesn't have a warm family relationship now. Wait until you are settled on your mission field. You can have a beautiful family involvement—as long as you nurture it and love it as the Bible says.

While on the mission field, missionaries most often assume the kinship relationship of brother and sister with the responsibilities and privileges afforded by those terms. Relationships are all important, especially in an Eastern, Oriental culture where everyone, it seems, is related to everyone else. In the Orient you find relationship terms and corresponding roles for people as far removed as your brother's son's wife's parents. A person in isolation is an anomaly in the East. Such a person is to be pitied, the concept being that even outcasts from society have some relatives to fall back on. So we become our colleagues' brothers and sisters. And, are we not? As children of the same Heavenly Father, we are brothers and sisters in Christ.

The brother/sister relationship helps to explain to nationals, or others who may wonder, why a man may have business with or be travelling with someone other than his own wife. There have been circumstances, as during wartime, when a mixed group have found themselves in very close living quarters, where they all have had to spend the night in the same room; when the call of nature must be answered in very primitive surroundings. All of this is easier to explain to questioning eyes and easier to laugh off yourself, if you think of your fellow worker as a big or little brother or sister.

If, however, we accept the pleasures of belonging to a large family, we must also be willing to accept the obligations entailed: loyalty, concern, help when needed, advice—all summed up in the word: love. The Bible gives the command, *"Let brotherly love continue,"* or as the N.I.V. gives it in Romans 12:10, *"Be devoted to one another in brotherly love."*

This will mean, at times, keeping your mouth shut, not divulging mission business to those outside the "family". It may mean sticking your neck out for somebody when he is in trouble. It always means showing at least the same respect and affection for this colleague brother or sister as you show, or ought to show, towards your own brothers and sisters.

Just as at home, it may be that on the mission field you are automatically more drawn to one person, one couple, one family than to some of the others. That is fine, but you need to try to get to know all the people with whom you live and work. This takes effort. It takes spending time together, both in the working situation and especially in the off duty hours. It means doing thoughtful little things for one another.

I never was much good at throwing mementos out and recently I came upon a note written on October 1, 1974. It was from the wife of the Senior missionary on our field and was addressed jointly to Lynn and me,

> "Today, my birthday, I was just sitting here and reminiscing about the goodness and greatness of God and some of the highlights of my life passed through my mind. One of those was that birthday when you two appeared at my door to take me for a surprise ride. Do you remember? I had just washed my hair and it was up on rollers. We rushed around to find somebody with a hair dryer so I could take it down. Then we drove to the newly opened hotel for 'high tea' in their coffee shop. That was lovely and is among my fond memories. I still appreciate it."

Every member of the missionary family needs to work at creating occasions which make warm memories and build up traditions.

One example is a Valentine's party the singles gave for the couples back in 1974. We held it in schoolteacher Sue Breckley's living room decorated with the appropriate hearts and flowers. As the guests arrived we entertained them with Lynn playing a small portable organ and me singing sentimental songs. The waiters then seated the couples at candlelit tables for two. Who were the waiters? Our one missionary bachelor, and an American engineer who had accepted Christ into his life during his association with us in Chittagong. With their black bow ties and a towel over their arms they looked the part perfectly. Bob, the engineer, had had menus printed with every exotic dish we could think of: pate de fois, pheasant under glass, and many more such. They soberly went from table to table writing down the diner's choice. Then they came out to the kitchen where Sue and I served up lasagne, the only dish we had prepared. The waiters took back the steaming squares of lasagne with the apology, "Sorry, we are all out of broasted cornish hen, (or whatever the order was), but would you like to try the speciality of the house?"

I went from table to table singing a song just for each couple—lines with the wife's name or a tune from home, e.g., "Mary" or "Carolina Moon." Some of the songs had to be fudged a bit as in the case of "Hello, Carol"!

We arranged for babysitters, and borrowed the projector and some educational films from the U.S. Information Service to round out the evening. Yes, it took a full day out of our regular duties, but it was worth it. These couples are still talking about that expression of love and appreciation for each other.

Anything we can do to nurture good interpersonal relations with our fellow workers is worthwhile. The Bible gives good counsel as to our relationship one with another,

> *"Brethren, you have been called unto liberty, only use not liberty for an occasion for the flesh, but by love serve one another. For all the law is fulfilled in this word, thou shalt love thy neighbor as thyself; but if you bite and devour one another take heed that ye be not consumed one of another."* (Galatians 5:13-15).

If we missionaries are brothers and sisters, what does that make us to the kids? It makes us aunt and uncle. "Auntie"—how I hated that expression my first term on the field! I must have driven people crazy by showing my repugnance for what to them was a very natural thing to say. But I had reason to dislike the term. I grew up in a pastor's home where many, many visitors passed through. Some of these people wanted to be called "aunt" or "uncle," or else my parents didn't know any better term for us to use, so I acquired many "aunts" and "uncles." To this day there are some people whom I never call by name because I don't know what to call them. To say "Rev. Hunt" to a family friend would be stilted and formal, and for me to say "Uncle George" now, sounds ridiculous. So I felt I had good reason not to lead another generation into the same problems I had faced. I thought this auntie and uncle business was foolish. But I matured and learned a few things that first term. I came to realize there are some basic values behind the practice of children calling adults "aunt" and "uncle." Kids need aunts and uncles. They are away from their own relatives and need this relationship. And—aunts and uncles need kids too! It works both ways.

The missionary community becomes in a degree the extended family which was the norm until recently in Western countries. In writing concerning the problems of the single parent trying to raise her children, Brenda Hunter says,

I came to see how imperative it is for children to have the larger family to relate to. Other adults flesh out the custodial parent's view of the world. In a shared life, children find what children in America found generations ago when relatives lived nearby to share in the child-rearing process. Since we transient Americans no longer have the extended family we must create our own larger family. The shared life of the Christian community can do this beautifully."[1]

Living in close contact with families, unmarried people have the joy of sharing in family living: holding new babies, watching little ones take their first steps, and introducing helpful dimensions into the children's lives.

There's also a practical reason for the aunt and uncle business. In many countries, the nationals would be horrified to hear a small child call an adult by his first name. This just is not done. At the same time to call someone you see regularly Mr. or Mrs. or Miss So-and-So gets a little ridiculous, too. Using aunt and uncle solves both problems.

As pleasant and helpful as this family relationship with its aunts and uncles can be, there are problems which can arise, caution flags which must be raised.

To the *unmarried*

Love these kids just as you do your own nieces and nephews. Spend time with them. Offer to take care of them so that their parents can go out on a date by themselves. You will find it helpful, if in preparing your outfit for your mission field, you include games, books, toys. Keep these in a special place in your house—on a book shelf, in a play box—that when the kids come to visit they will know they are welcome. They will know you have thought about them and planned for them. However, in establishing a play area and toys to play with, be sure you set rules. You may want to set specific times when the children are allowed to come. That prevents untimely running in and out. If there are particular items you don't want touched, explain that to older children and "babyproof" the room for little ones by removing the fragile objects. If you don't want them playing a musical instrument that is in your house or turning on certain appliances, tell them. Make sure they know what their limits are. And expect them to abide by your rules while they are in your house. You are the adult and this is your home.

In many areas of living, but perhaps more in this area of dealing with children than in any other, the rule, "know your place" applies. Certain areas fall exclusively within the rights of parents, and the unmarried person does well to back away gracefully from them. Never correct or discipline a child when his own parents are present. If the rules of your house are being broken, tell the parent or remove the offending item or focus of trouble, but don't reprove or punish someone else's child.

Be very careful to remember these are not your own children. They have their own parents. And their parents have particular standards and rules of conduct which they allow. No outsider has the right to interfere. But we can volunteer to help when help is needed.

In 1971 Bangladesh underwent a civil and then an international war. All but three of our missionaries were required to evacuate the country (as were many from other Mission Boards). The group I was in was composed of 13 adults and 21 children. We traveled by Landrover, sampan, army truck, P.T. boat and plane on our route from Chittagong, Bangladesh through Burma and down to Bangkok. But that's all another story! I remember at one hold-over point, American Embassy personnel came to our rescue with food and cold drinks. As we three singles: nurse Becky Davey, Lynn Silvernale and I were helping to corral the children on to the next means of transport, one Embassy attache remarked, "These kids obey you just as if you were their parents."

Then at the Christian and Missionary Alliance Guest House in Bangkok where we lived as refugees for a few weeks, the kindly Guest House manager would come to ask us, "What planned activity do you have for the children today?", (which being interpreted was, "When will we have a little peace around here?") The children did respond to us. We had then, and still have, a very happy relationship with them, but they are not our kids. We must guard against violating any principles their own parents hold. We must be careful not to pit child against parent or one child against another.

In spiritual areas too, it is wrong to usurp the parent's place. A group of Bangladesh missionaries was worshipping together at a Sunday evening service in another country. During the meeting, a number of school children returning from their year in boarding stood to give testimonies of what God had done in their lives. Various ones told of accepting Christ as Saviour, or of winning spiritual victories. Each one praised the houseparents, the staff, the teachers of the school for the part those people had played in their lives. Following the service, one of our group, a mother of three wistfully said, "I want to have those experiences with my children myself."

I don't think she was being selfish. I think she was speaking for her

God-given right and duty. She and her husband had been given those three children. The responsibility for their spiritual birth and growth is every bit as much theirs as that of the children's physical development. That does not mean there will never be times when the housemother, the teacher, the "auntie" is not exactly the right person to talk with the child. Sometimes problems of distance, of inter-communication difficulties or the emergency of the situation will demand that the person at hand be the one to guide the child. But when the child's own parents are present, they are the ones who ought to have the privilege of leading their own children to Christ, of teaching them God's design for love, sex and marriage, of guiding them in decision making for the future.

To the *married*

Never just assume that "auntie" will take your kids. Never take it for granted that the single people don't have much to do, so of course they can baby-sit. Wait for them to make the offer or, if the singles don't even know you need a baby sitter, ask if it is possible for them to help just then. Ask as nicely as you would ask of an outsider from whom you needed help.

Sometimes unmarried people invite the children in by themselves without their parents. This can be a special treat for both: kids get to eat out and the parents get an evening to themselves! Over the years traditions have built up in various places. For example, on one mission station the children always go to the single ladies house for an evening of Christmas cookie decoration. Other places have regular Hallowe'en or Valentine's Day parties.

When a special invitation comes for the children, don't put down the person doing the inviting by saying, "Oh, you don't know my kids. You could never handle them!" That is a back-handed insult. If she didn't think she could handle them, she would never have invited them in the first place. Don't assume she won't be able to manage your kids. "Thank you" is the proper response to an invitation like that.

"Children are a heritage from the Lord." Whether they are your very own or those you have adopted by dint of joining a mission family, they are precious. Children enrich the lives of everyone. One of the extras of missionary service among a group of colleagues is, I have found, the joy of close association with the children, our adopted family.

[1]Brenda Hunter, *Beyond Divorce: A Personal Journey* (Old Tappan: Fleming H. Revell, 1978)

Chapter Three

Learning To Be Content

Every newcomer to our Bangladesh field is given on arrival an orientation packet. Heeded and followed it becomes invaluable in the developing of an effective, fruitful missionary. Along with the practical aspects—purchasing, banking, customs and culture—is a section on the vital importance of learning to adjust to one's situation, of finding the Will of God to be acceptable. One section is entitled, "The Single Person's Adjustment to the mission field." This excellent article was written by veteran missionary Mary Lou Brownwell, and it is to her I am indebted for many of the insights in this chapter. In her article, she draws material from the book, *Hind's Feet in High Places,* by Hannah Hurnard; and with permission of the publisher I quote:

> It is God's will that some of His children should learn deep union with Himself through the perfect flowering of natural human love in marriage. For others it is equally His will that the same perfect union should be learnt through the experience of learning to lay down completely this natural and instinctive desire for marriage and parenthood, and the circumstances of life which deny them this experience . . . The only way is by learning to accept day by day, the actual conditions and tests permitted by God, by a continual repeated laying down of our own will and acceptance of His as it is presented to us in the form of the people with whom we have to live and work, and in the things that happen to us.[1]

No missionary—for that matter no person—will find satisfaction or be able to achieve God's best for him if he is constantly chafing at his lot in life.

There are many frustrations over which a person, especially one living in a foreign country, has no control: endless government red tape, stifling bureaucracy that slows down every advancement, inefficiency perhaps brought on by the climate and poor nutrition, shortages of water, electricity and basic necessities, excessive heat or cold or rain, a pestering wind that blows dirt through the house whooshing carefully weighted down papers and whirling them about. But all of those, and a host of other inconveniences can be taken in stride if underneath there is the basic foundational belief: this is where God wants me to be. I can and will be happy here. Andrew Murray left us his formula for a contented spirit:

> "I am here by God's appointment
> In His keeping
> Under His training
> For His time."

The concept that I am here in these circumstances by God's design needs to be more than a "grin and bear it" attitude. There must be joy in being and doing what it is that God has called us to do. Without the joy, the long hours become unmitigated toil, the frustrations become misery. I don't think God intends that service for Him be drudgery. Christ Himself said, *"The thief cometh not, but for to steal and to destroy. I am come that they might have life and that they might have it more abundantly"* (John 10:10).

The thief, Satan, would try to rob the Christian worker of his usefulness by destroying his sense of joy. Jesus prayed for His followers that *"their joy may be full"* (John 16:24).

The missionary or Christian worker who is performing his duties merely out of obligation, without enjoyment, might do well to re-evaluate his present area of service. When God calls to a place or to a particular work, He undergirds with joy. That is most certainly not to say that He allows only a smooth road, all lightness and air. No, the outward circumstances may be hard, very hard. There may be illness, pain, separation from loved ones, lack of interest on the part of the people in the homelands who promised to support you by prayer and gifts. And even harder than those, there may be disappointments in the very work you are doing. Others may write home about scores of "souls saved" and your ones and twos seem to be slipping backwards. In other countries new churches are springing up faster than the Church Growth charts; your struggling church is fractious and barely alive. You teach your heart out on matters of Christian living, only to have your finest leaders agree wholeheartedly but then remark that they will "return to what we are habituated to do." You exert yourself to raise a family from abject poverty. You treat them medically, find a job, put the children in school, locate a better living environment—and the man robs you blind! You labor over an inquirer, lead him to Christ, painstakingly guide him in his first steps, breathe a sign of relief as he seems firm and grounded in the faith—only to have him slip back to his old religion for the expediency of a job or marriage.

These are not joyous experiences. They cause heartache, disappointment, discouragement. Even with the distressing conditions, however, there can be an underlying sense of contentment. I don't know *how* it works, but I know it does! Contentment says—this place, these circumstances are right for me at this time. This must be more than a head knowledge, more than lip service to a bunch of platitudes. It must be a fact upon which you build your life. The Apostle Paul wrote, *"Godliness with contentment is great gain"* (I Timothy 6:6). And even Paul admitted he had to learn that. (Phil. 4:11). Being content was not something that came naturally.

I have known this feeling of contentment many times since arriving in Bangladesh. One instance that stands out in my memory happened during my second year as a missionary here. My language teacher had come for my daily class from 6:00 to 7:00 A.M. Never much of a morning person, I had again foggily recited my way through a reading assignment. By 8:00 A.M., ten squiggly pre-schoolers and kindergarteners were on my front verandah for the nursery school I conducted, which allowed their parents to spend the morning in language study. If you have had ten one-to-five year olds around all at once, you'll know the chaos of the morning. If you haven't you wouldn't understand even if I told you.

We were planning a fancy dinner party for that evening. Along with the meat and potatoes part, I had one hoarded tin of vegetables and a real treat: a newly arrived cake mix only six months or so old from its voyage halfway around the world. I had visions of a high chocolate layer cake with mounds of fluffy seven minute frosting. At mid-morning, cookie and Kool-aid time, the cook called me to the kitchen. Remember, I hadn't wanted that cook in the first place. Only when I learned that a woman does not do her own marketing in this Muslim culture, and when I saw the meat hanging by its haunches and the live chickens flapping their wings at me, did I realize the necessity for a cook.

Wishing to surprise me and save me the work of the cake and the frosting, he had done it all himself and was now calling me to praise his handiwork. There on the counter sat my lovely cake. It was in a sheet pan and was as flat as the smoothest military sheet. And the icing! The toothless old cook grinned as he pointed to all the colors he had been able to conjure up out of the four little food coloring bottles. My white mountain frosting had turned into Joseph's coat! Suspiciously I then lifted a lid from a pot on the stove. Boiling happily away was all the popcorn from a tin I had hidden to pop for nibble food later in the evening. The cook complained it had been boiling for three hours—why wasn't it getting soft?

A ruined cake—a houseful of squalling kids—inconvenient language study! Life was awful! I let out one cry, "Lord, help me! Suddenly almost perceptibly, I was engulfed in comfort while the Lord seemed to say, "It's okay. I brought you here. I'll bring you through."

Then I started to laugh. Wait till the people tonight see that cake! And what a letter home the popcorn episode will make! I started back to the porch. Yes, Debbie and Mark were still fighting over the paint brushes. Linda was mashing cookies all over the floor and Marty was a mess; but it was alright. This was the place to be, the work to do—for me at this time. The Lord filled me with His contentment and peace.

Where does contentment come from? Can it be worked up by fervent prayer and soul searching? Is it dished out at conferences and retreats? Is it a spiritual grace to be sought after? In my experience the answer to each of these would be "No." Contentment comes as Amy Carmichael, missionary to India for over 55 years wrote, "In acceptance lieth peace." Contentment comes as Hannah Hurnard wrote, "by learning to accept day by day."

But even the acceptance is not to be made with a gritting of your teeth, or by maintaining "a stiff upper lip." Rather, the acceptance of circumstances that brings contentment is that which is accompanied with gladness. Not a silly, "Praise the Lord, I broke my leg." Not the pious tones we used at the cafeteria during nurses' training days, "Thank you Lord for these wretched powdered eggs," but as we find in Psalms and Proverbs,

"Thou has put gladness in my heart" (Pslam 4:7).
"A merry heart maketh a cheerful countenance" (Proverbs 15:13).
A merry heart doeth good like a medicine" (Proverbs 17:22).

In her allegory, *Hinds' Feet on High Places,* Hannah Hurnard follows the life of "Much-Afraid" as she leaves her apprehensive relatives and travels to the high Place of Victory with the Good Shepherd. Part of her journey takes her through a desert. She writes,

In all that great desert, there was not a single green thing growing, neither tree, nor flower, nor plant save here and there a patch of straggly grey cacti.

On the last morning she was walking near the tents and huts of the desert dwellers, when in a lonely corner behind a wall she came upon a little golden yellow flower, growing all alone. An old pipe was connected with a water tank. In the pipe was one tiny hole through which came an occasional drop of water. Where the drops fell one by one, there grew the little golden flower, though where the seed had come from, Much-Afraid could not imagine for there were no birds anywhere and no other growing things.

She stooped over the lonely, lovely little golden face, lifted up so hopefully and so bravely to the feeble drip and cried out softly, "What is your name little flower, for I never saw one like you before."

The tiny plant answered at once, in a tone as golden as itself, "Behold me! My name is Acceptance-with-Joy." [2]

One of the biggest obstacles to a life of contentment is envy of another person: his position, marital status, gifts, opportunities. We never seem to envy another person's trials, do we? Yet these might be what has made the person what he is.

In your list of do's and don'ts, write in large letters: Don't be jealous. Don't clog up your mind with, "Why them—not us?", "Why her—not me?"

"Why?" is a defeat producing word. An *unmarried woman* may ask "Why does she have somebody to love her? Why does she have someone to take care of her while I don't? It's not fair. Why did this happen to me?" Those kind of "whys" just waste your time and energy. Paul said unmarried people would have more time to serve the Lord, but that's not true if you're constantly asking, "Why am I single? Why don't I have a husband?" If you are spending your time complaining, scheming, plotting, accusing God, then all that time Paul said you would have is gone, dissipated in useless emotional energy.

The issue of marriage or not, or the timing of that marriage is one which is best left in God's hands to work out. The Pslamist wrote,

"He shall choose our inheritance" (Psalm 47:4). Charles Spurgeon expanded on this by saying, "Had any other condition been better for you than the one in which you find yourself, divine love would have placed you there."

It's good to remember that. God has put you where you are because He loves you and wants the very best for you. I get sick and tired of a particular type of book which makes good story telling, but is not true. The missionary accounts go like this:

Girl says to God, "I will go to the mission field only if you give me a husband." After a struggle she comes to the point of surrender where she says, "Alright Lord, I am willing to go to the mission field without a husband." Bingo—husband!

In such books, it's as if you get a plum at the end for having said, "I surrender to God." If it is in God's plan for you to have a husband, God will arrange it. Remember God loves you very, very much. There is a beautiful verse which reinforces that assurance, *"I know the plans I have for you, plans to prosper you and not to harm you, plans to give you hope and a future"* (Jeremiah 29:11 N.I.V.).

Rather than frustrating yourself with trying to figure out the unfathomable "whys", spend your time in cultivating contentment and peace.

A man highly respected, and much beloved in the circle of Baptists with which my mission is associated was Dr. Robert T. Ketcham. He also happens to be the father of our fellow worker, Dr. Donn Ketcham. The elder Dr. Ketcham coined a phrase which has carried many of us through dark hours:

> "Your Heavenly Father is too good to be unkind and too wise to make mistakes."

Write that on your wall, on your mirror, in your heart and believe it.

Above all, don't allow the "whys", the questions which you cannot answer to become a root of bitterness in your life. Don't let bitterness strangle your love, and joy and happiness. I first found the following poem signed anonymously, then later credited to Natalie Ray. Read these poignant words carefully and take them to heart, especially if resentment toward God is eating away at you because you feel you have been refused what you think is your heart's desire.

> No lover makes my kiss his daily quest
> No hand across the table reaches mine.

No precious baby nestles at my breast.
No one to need my love. Where is the sign
That God, my Father loves me? Surely He
Creates this wealth of love to overflow.
How can it be that no one who wanted me
Has become mine? Why did I tell them 'no'?
But do they really matter—all the 'Why's'?
Could all the answers take away the pain,
Or all the reasons really dry my eyes,
Though sent from Heaven's courts?
No, I would weep again.
My God, You have saved me from Hell's black abyss;
Oh, save me from the tyranny of bitterness!

A Wycliffe missionary in the Philippines was a classmate of one of my colleagues in Bangladesh. She writes breezy letters about her work which we all enjoy reading. In commenting about a book she had recently read concerning the unmarried state, she wrote, "I really don't think being single is all that awful. I've certainly enjoyed it. But maybe I've been more fortunate than most in that I have always had good friends in the same boat with none of us sitting around crying about it." That's contentment—with joy.

In my experience, the *married gals'* "Whys?" polarize at two extremes. The one says, "Why do I have to go to language school? Why do I have to learn the language? I'm not going to be preaching and teaching. I am going to be taking care of my house and family. Why are these difficult requirements for me?"

I will let a missionary mother from the Philippines speak to this point,

Fellow-wives and mothers, I'd like to interject a special word about our part in this enterprise. When we joined the mission together with our husbands, we came out with the full knowledge that we were coming as missionaries. (There are some mission boards under which only the husbands function as missionaries.) And did you realize we get the same salary as our husbands? Frankly I think our job is harder than that of the men: we are called to be wives first, mothers second, and missionaries third. It is no easy matter to correlate these three roles. But the Lord has not asked us to do anything for which He will not empower us. And we *did* come as missionaries. If we were in the States, we'd be doing all our own cooking, dishes, cleaning, washing, ironing and marketing. If the Lord has provided us with household help for these jobs, we will not be spending any *less* time with our children because of doing missionary work here, than we would be in the States.

We certainly are not called upon to conduct evangelistic campaigns but listen to the words of William Carey: "In conversing with the wives of native converts, and leading them on in the ways of Christ, so that they may be an ornament to the Christian cause, and make known the Gospel to the native women, we hope always to have the assistance of the females who have embarked with us in the mission. It behooves us therefore, to afford to our European sisters all possible assistance in acquiring the language, that they may, in every way that Providence may open to them, become instrumental in prompting the salvation of the millions of native women who are in a great measure excluded from all opportunities of hearing the Word from the mouths of European men."

Could it be that our language learning is attacked so fiercely because the devil knows that we need to know it in order to be the most effective missionaries?[3]

Yes, it is difficult to leave those little ones while you go off to language school. It is hard to keep your mind on past active participles when you have been up all night with a crying baby. It is heartrending to send the school-age children away to boarding school during the academic year. Hard—yes; impossible—no. Mothers from many fields testify as to how thankful they are that they were encouraged—or forced—to spend time in language study when they first arrived. One mother of four wrote, "Being a missionary mother and learning a new language will never be an easy or a comfortable thing, but it is very necessary."

As with the unmarried woman these frustrations too can be helped by accepting the fact: "This is where God has placed me now. This is my responsibility. I will accept it. I will accept it with joy."

When a group of parents on our Bangladesh field were engrossed in language study, they were encouraged by members of our mission studying Chinese in Hong Kong. The encouragement came in the form of a poem which we freely admit plagiarizing. Here is the Bengali adaptation:

The rains have come, the weather's hot
The ayah broke the coffeepot.
Donn just fired my new mali
Forget it all and learn Bengali.

Chittagong shampoo is up in cost
What we had in the barrel's lost.
Cockroaches fighting on the drape—
Concentrate on tomorrow's tape.

Rain is coming under the door,
Water's covered the bathroom floor
It doesn't mean a thing to me—
Today's a quiz on lesson three.

That broken door still will not lock
And Kitty smashed the bedroom clock.
What else did Donn intend to say?
A test on characters today?

Another bulb must be replaced
Marty's in my brand new paste!
How can I do conversation
And revise today's translation?

Home is 12,000 miles away
Frustrations multiply each day
When you're feeling glum and growly—
Forget it all—just learn Bengali.

At the other end of the pole of "Why's?", the married woman feels, "This isn't fair. God called me to be a missionary, too. I went forward in a consecration service. I dedicated my life to the Lord. Why do I have to be stuck in this house all the time? All I ever do is take care of the kids."

The frustration this brings can lead to as much bitterness as can be felt by the woman with no children to care for. It could cause the mother to leave her children with unsuitable nationals where the child may learn unfit language, unsanitary or immoral practices. Or it may cause her to continually dump her children on some fellow-worker's doorstep while she goes out to "do the Lord's work."

Again the solution to the problem boils down to those words, "acceptance with joy" of the situation in which you find yourself. If there are small children at home, spend time with them. They are little for such a short while. All too soon you will want to hold them or give them a hug, and they are too grown up for all that "nonsense." Use your time wisely. (This will be discussed in a later chapter.) There will be times when the children are sleeping or playing safely or in school, when you can engage in other activities for the Lord.

Remember that these children whom you may think are keeping you from missionary work, might well be the actual entrance into a home. When you take them along, or even just talk about homemaking and children, about 50% of your introduction battle is over because you are relating to the local people. Unmarried people sometimes have a harder time getting a conversation going in visiting in a new area. Invariably people ask about your husband and children. The conversation goes like this:

"What does your husband do?"
"You don't *have* a husband!"
"Have you no parents: did they not arrange a marriage for you?"

My colleague Mary Lou Brownell has her classic answer to the husband question. She sweetly replies, "My husband died at birth." For those of you who do not need to use an answer like that, praise God for your husband and children and for the entre they give you into people's homes.

The married lady missionary's frustrations increase when the problem seems compounded by, "I'm stuck here at home with these kids and some other woman is working with *my* husband."

On this point, words of caution are in order to the unmarried women and in some circumstances to the married women as well: *"Abstain from all appearance of evil"* (I Thessalonians 5:22).

If you are working with someone else's husband, be sure everything about the relationship is above board. Be sure the doors are wide open and everyone can see what is going on in that office or room. Do not give any cause for suspicion either to that person's wife or to national staff or to anyone.

Unless it is absolutely necessary, don't ride in a car or travel alone with someone else's husband. If his wife cannot go along on that trip, take a missionary colleague, a national or a child. Do not give occasion for any kind of suspicion. In Bangladesh very definitely, and in many other cultures, it is not considered possible for a person to live a pure moral life alone. So immediately when the nationals see a man and a woman in deep discussion or in close proximity they assume that they are either married or somebody is up to no good. Avoid suspicion at all costs.

Quite likely it will happen that you will be involved in a project with someone else's husband. A nurse in a hospital, a teacher in a school, etc. Remember, men often get completely involved in their work. They have a good idea and they want to get on with it. They forget that back home with the kids, half of the team hasn't heard about this particular project. The wives, who may not be present, need to be included in the discussion and be allowed to give their ideas on matters of general concern. Try not to make major decisions during coffee break time at the office or at a time when all of the team is not present.

Wives, remember there are times when teachers, doctors, nurses have to talk about their particular field. Be understanding. don't make a big thing of it when your husband and a lady colleague have business matters to discuss—even when they use professional jargon that you might not understand. Many a good working relationship has been ruined by a wife who was jealous when there was no cause for it. It's ridiculous for her to assume that because an unmarried colleague casually passes the time of day with her husband, she must have designs on him. The wife who is so insecure needs help to work through this problem. This is likewise true of the married man who misreads normal working interaction as a woman having ulterior motives.

The wife, however, who feels she does have cause to be concerned about another person's relationship with her husband, needs to get to the root of the problem—fast. Talk it out with him or go and see the woman. If neither of these seems possible, a third party should be called on to help. Don't let Satan get the upper hand here. He would love to tear a marriage apart under the guise of two people dedicated to their work.

Conversely, if you are in the position of working closely with another woman's husband, don't assume his wife is jealous of you. I remember nearly getting myself into a mess over this very thing. Early in the days when I was learning what was involved in starting and directing a literature ministry, I was privileged to attend a literature management conference in Singapore. A missionary man from another mission and a Bengali colleague also had been invited. We met in Bangladesh's capital city and travelled to Singapore and back together. Three months after the Singapore conference I met the missionary and his wife at a series of special meetings. He and I began to talk about the trip, of interesting incidents and experiences we had shared. Admittedly, it was rude to discuss things that others in the conversation did not know about, but there had been nothing in our relationship which we would have been embarrassed to tell his wife. Later in the day I found the wife crying softly to herself in a corner of the church. My first thought was to rush to her and explain away things that had never happened. I am eternally grateful I had the sense to keep my mouth shut. She, as a mature woman, had accepted her husband's business trip and the associations it developed. She was crying because they had just put their three children on the plane to enter boarding school 1100 miles away.

So far we've been focusing mostly on women, married or otherwise. But now a word to the men. Sometimes actions or words that you are in the habit of using can innocently get you and others into trouble. For example, I was in a shoe store in New York City and a man I'd never seen before called me "darling" as I walked in. In many places endearing terms: "honey, love, sweetheart" are used without second thought. Be careful of these words if you are a man who uses them casually. They probably don't mean a thing to you. But there are a couple of reasons why you need to watch the way you address women. In most countries American movies have preceded you, and nationals know what words like darling, honey, sweetheart imply. When they hear you say these words to someone other than your wife, they are going to suspect something however innocent you are. A good rule is: take those words out of your vocabulary as concerning anyone outside of your family.

Some men are friendly types who come up to a girl and put an arm around her or pat her as a greeting. Beware of that with anyone but your own family also. Besides how it may look to watching nationals, there is another reason for restraint: the girl you are calling "dear" or "sweetie-pie" or patting on the shoulder may be feeling particularly lonely. She may take your expression in entirely the wrong way. You might have meant absolutely nothing by it. You might call the cat by the same term, but the girl might pick up your words or gestures and build someting which you never intended. Watch your speech and the way you conduct yourself around women.

Remember the *Don't* book mentioned in the first chapter? Here is a quote from it that still has merit today in the context of men and women relationships especially in a foreign country,

"Don't be over-familiar. Don't slap your friends on the back, nudge them in the side, or give any other physical manifestation of your pleasure in seeing them."

In many countries a man not only has to be careful about his actions and speech around his colleagues, but even the way he conducts himself with his wife in public is a matter for concern.

A number of years ago a new missionary family were moving to their primitive jungle station. The whole process of transporting food, household goods and three small children had been a nightmare from the beginning. The day's problems culminated in their low-lying country boat being stuck and stranded all night on a sand bar. After settling the children down, the thoughtful husband put his arm around his wife in a gesture of comfort. What they didn't know was that this was highly offensive behavior to the nationals accompanying them on the boat. For a long time their testimony was hindered by this private gesture carried out in a way which the nationals thought was degrading to a woman.

Another young pair were walking a narrow mound of dirt between rice paddies en route to an interior village. The husband playfully kept stepping on his wife's rubber thong as she preceded him on the path. She stood it as long as she could and then in an exasperated moment she swatted him one with her sandal. Word of her insubordination and especially of her using such a disrespectful and defiled object as a *shoe,* traveled to the village faster than the missionaries did and severely hindered their acceptance there.

The social mores vary greatly from country to country. Yours might be a place where everyone kisses everyone on sight. That also takes some adjusting to! The point being, that until you are very sure who it is socially correct to touch, keep your hands to yourself.

But the main subject here is contentment, accepting with joy the circumstances and situations in which you find yourself. These situations may be different from what you are used to. They may be funny or frustrating, unusual or unsettling. Whatever they are, they are what your loving Lord chooses for you at this point in your life. Did you notice that sentence is in the present tense? Too many people merely endure life now, existing in the vague hope that somehow things will be better in the future. Don't waste your life doing that, rather—LIVE IN THE NOW.

Life is here to be lived now. We all are so time oriented. We slot things away to be done at the right time. Often in waiting for the right time, we lose out on the enjoyment, the adventures of the NOW. It starts in childhood, this constant looking forward to the future. "What are you going to be when you grow up?" everyone asks, not remembering that right now, the little one can be a pilot, a nurse or a fireman or an engineer—or all of these together, all by means of the imagination.

We all have it, this breathless feeling, "When such and such happens, then . . ." When I was in nurses' training, we draped safety pins around the room indicating the number of months, then weeks, then days until it was over. Innocent enough, I suppose, yet I wonder if I made the most of those three years which in retrospect were among the happiest of my life in terms of living, learning and loving.

Many girls turn down invitations to be part of a group attending a play, a concert, a game because they don't have a date. Granted, it is delightful to have a special companion and often the service given to unescorted women in restaurants is appalling, but don't let that keep you at home if the event is something you would enjoy. In fact, if the occasion is something which interests you greatly, go—even if it means going alone. Better to be sitting alone enjoying the program, than merely to be sitting at home alone. Do what you enjoy doing. Do it now. Don't wait until some dim, distant future when your circumstances might be changed.

Buy or make what is necessary to make your living quarters a home. Use your creative abilities or borrow the skills of a friend. Don't fall into the mind-set that thinks, "If this were our own house, we'd make it look better," or "If I were married I'd fix the place up a bit." That room, or those rooms are where God placed you NOW; make the most of them.

Elisabeth Elliot who has experienced so much in terms of missionary service and living as a single person, a widow and a wife, says:

"Let not our longing slay the appetite of our living. Accept and thank God for what is given not allowing the not-given to spoil it."

Therein is contentment.

[1]Hannah Hurnard, *Hind's Feet in High Places* (Wheaton: Tyndale House, 1975), pages 6, 7.

[2]*Ibid,* pages 76, 77.

[3]Mrs. Henry DeVries, Jr., "A Matter of Motivation", by permission.

[4]Harry Ambacher, "Forget It All—And Learn Chinese," adapted.

Chapter Four

The Importance of Being Friendly

As a teenager growing up in Brooklyn, part of my social life centered around the ice cream parlor. "Parlor" pronounced without the first "r"—as only a New Yorker would do! Whether the occasion was a date, with a group from the church after choir practice, or a bunch of student nurses escaping from Pharmacology class for a while, the purpose was the same: fun, fellowship, companionship. The food made very little difference—I don't even like ice cream! The point was being together. The ice cream parlors that stand out best in my memory are the quaint, family operated ones with an aura of the early 1900's about them. But there's a chain of ice cream shops in New York that brings into focus the reason we visited those restaurants. The chain is called Friendly's.

Being friendly is a key to good relationships wherever one may be. Having accepted God's place for you at this time, then the challenge comes to live out that situation to its fullest. Since most people are sociable by nature, the enjoyment of a job or position or calling is often related to the friends they find, or rather *make* along the way. For the making or keeping of friends is a working proposition, a continuous process. Proverbs 18:24 states, *"A man that hath friends must show himself friendly."* Friendship is a two-way street.

A missionary in a foreign country has unusual opportunities to practice the art of friendship. As you become more and more acquainted with the nationals in your country, your life is enriched by experiences shared with them.

There are times though when you feel the need to be with people more or less from your own background. You have your missionary family, of course, but it is profitable to cultivate friends outside your own group. In many countries there are people serving with a variety of missionary agencies. This is an avenue for personal friendships. Because of differing beliefs and convictions you may not choose to join in their spiritual programs, but you certainly can eat popcorn and pizza with them. Besides missionaries, there may be business people, foreign students, diplomatic or AID or Peace Corps personnel—a variety of people to associate with.

In Bangladesh I have been invited to receptions for ambassadors, to parties for Officers of the Fleet, to social gatherings with visiting dignitaries from many places.

One annual function always amused us: the Farm Association sponsored a yearly trip to Third World countries and Chittagong, Bangladesh was included on the itinerary. The USAID people who hosted the party must have felt that their guests from the Bible belt would feel more at home with missionaries than with the AID people's usual cocktail party friends, so every year came our invitation to the Farmer's Dinner.

So we do have a social life even though Chittagong has been called by many people "the absolute end of the world!" I can think of many nights in Chittagong when there were four, five or more English or American bachelors sitting around the table in the house where Lynn and I lived. They were teachers, engineers, students, business men—all living overseas on two or three year assignments.

To the individual or the couple who are at all outgoing, there is scope for a wide range of friendships. There is even a possibility for evangelism in these contacts. All of the young men at our table heard the Gospel. Some have gone on to live for the Lord. But with all the pleasure and even the potential which these friendships provide, there must be a note of warning sounded for the missionary. A missionary group needs to carefully discuss the matter and set goals and priorities in regards to involvement with the foreign community. If it is in the scope of your mission's plans and personnel to conduct a program for them, then regular co-mingling is essential. If, however, your priority is to establish a national church in the national language, then most of the missionary's time and effort must be in that direction and contacts with foreigners kept to pleasant, but less frequent intervals.

Isobel Kuhn serving with Overseas Missionary Fellowship, addressed this problem when she and her husband pioneered in Northern Thailand after they had been forced to leave China.

In every civilized city of the Orient, there is a thing called the White Community. The color of your skin elects you to its membership whether you like it or not. In Chiengmai it will give you a Welcome Party—just merry games and nice refreshments, and get-to-know-everybody. For those who are tied down all day to busy schedules (the secretary's desk, the schoolroom, the hospital beds), it offers relaxation. If you embrace it warmly, you will soon find yourself in a social whirl. It may seem harmless and everybody is so nice you hate to refuse; you seem like a piker to refuse invitations, but nevertheless there it is—the Whirl. Very soon John and I had to face the question: How much time were we going to spend at parties and social teas?

Speaking from the mere relaxation side of it, we felt that we OMFers did not need it. We were none of us institutional workers and our lives were far from monotonous. We had plenty of variety. But there was another angle to it—the indigenus pattern to which we were pledged. This suggests that relaxation times should be spent with the nationals. Do we need a game of volleyball? Call in the Thai neighbors to take part. The same holds for parties and picnics. Thai friends are always available. This does not mean we never went to a party; it means that this was the pattern to which we felt committed.[1]

In considering the friendships you make outside of your own mission group, there are two dangers to be avoided:

1. You can spend all of your time with "outside" people to the exclusion of your own missionary family.

As we said in a previous chapter, your missionary family is the group of people into which God has placed you at this time. God chose that roommate, that couple next door, that family to work with—for you at this time. He put you in proximity so you could learn specific lessons from one another. You can thwart this purpose of God by always running off with another crowd.

2. You can become so involved in keeping up friendships and maintaining a social calendar that you neglect the work and the reason for which you came to the mission field in the first place.

In 1963 I went to East Pakistan as it was then. I was occupied with full time language study for the first year, but by June 1964, I hadn't made much progress. I didn't have time to. I was having too much fun—remember those bachelors mentioned earlier? In that month of June, one of our mission executives came for a routine visit. Before his visit was over he called me for an interview and announced in a gracious, but firm tone that I would be leaving the city of Chittagong and moving up to our jungle station where I could study minus the distractions. Although I fussed and fumed at the time, I am sure I would never have learned the language had I not made that move.

The men were fun to have around. They were a happy diversion to counter balance the stresses of language study. I will always look back on those days with fond memories of dinners and games and parties. But each moved on when his tour of duty was over. God had called me to stay, to work with the people of Bangladesh. In order to do that it was essential to have a foundation of the language, the customs and culture.

For *single women* this area of male companionship—or the lack of it—is one which can cause much frustration. Some people seem able to settle this issue before they ever come to the field. It would never occur to them even to suppose there would be opportunities for such friendships on the mission field. Others struggle with it daily.

This brings up the whole area of dating on the mission field. Be sensible about this issue. Who can be sensible about dating? At least be reasonable! Some girls bewail the fact that because they are on the mission field they don't have any dates. Who is to say they would be dating if they were back home? Think of all the girls you know who do not date—not because they are thousands of miles away from home, but because there is no one suitable to date among their acquaintances. Don't feel you have been cheated out of dating and the possibility of getting married because you have chosen to serve the Lord in a foreign land. I have received many letters from women in the States in this vein:

> Perhaps you could tell me how you find it as a single woman in your circumstances. What do you do about the human, natural cravings for affection, love and attention. I hope you don't mind my asking these personal questions that I am coping with. I am 26 and single and I crave tender, loving care.

In answering her, I wrote,

> I have no pat answers for you because there are no easy answers. I can only share with you what I have found to be helpful. My underlying conscious feeling is that God loves me and knows what is best for me. This is more than just pretty phrases. I have seen it work so many times. I get an idea in my head and I scheme and plan and struggle and the whole thing flops, but when I turn it over to the Lord, He has a way of

working it all out. When I think back to the times when I asked, or even demanded of the Lord that He give me this person or that thing the way I wanted, I shudder. The only way I have found to have joy and fulfillment is to concentrate on doing what the Lord wants me to do now, at this moment in the circumstances in which He has put me. Leave the future entirely in His hands. Don't ask me how it works. I just know that when you stop plotting and designing, God takes over. He then gives peace and contentment.

Before blaming God and the mission field for your lack of dates, take a careful look at your definition of a date. If every social event must be a romantic encounter and every man a marriage prospect, then you are in for trouble. Still you can enjoy fun, fellowship and rewarding experiences on a friendship basis. Remember the proverb, *"A man to have friends must show himself friendly"*? Showing oneself friendly—not being a designing female—takes time and effort. It means keeping up correspondences, fitting in visits as and when the friends happen to be in the same place (sometimes that means when in even the same continent) and being ready to fit in to another person's equally busy schedule. Seminars, business lunches, meetings, group activities, while perhaps not as exciting as a candle-lit dinner for two, still can be fun "dates."

It's not only the single people who need to revise their definition of a date. Sometimes the married folk nip a friendship in the bud by reading more into it than exists at that moment. I remember a young widower from another mission who came for a visit to our hospital. Among the American staff was a girl he had met once before. Hoping to get to know her better, he invited her to play tennis with him. Before the first set was finished, all the married matchmakers on the compound had them engaged. The man soon went on to Hong Kong and married a lady from his mission there.

Closely tied in with the matter of dating, of letting friendships follow their natural course, is the problem of teasing. Teasing, of course is part of family life. We tease each other about many things, but sometimes the teasing can take on a barbed twist. I often think the husbands are more guilty of this than are the wives. Many men always seem to have something to say about a girl's getting married or not. Be careful about flippant remarks. You don't know what the girl you are talking to has gone through in the past. You don't know the person or proposal she turned down so she could be just where she is right now. You don't know but that she is currently corresponding, weighing the issue: shall I stay here and do this work, or shall I go home and marry him? Your remarks probably spoken in jest can cause a lot of hurt.

One of our Bangladesh missionaries told of a situation in a language school in India. In the school with our missionary nurse was a lovely new missionary girl from New Zealand. It was common knowledge that a young man also from New Zealand would be joining the class. Everyone assumed, "John is coming. Here is your husband on his way." She built up wonderful dreams in her mind. John arrived. He never once looked at the young girl from New Zealand. He married a lady from another country who was ten years older than he. That couple has had a very happy life, but the New Zealander girl went home broken hearted. People had made so much of a non-existent situation. They had teased her into believing something that wasn't to be. Teasing is fun, but be sure it doesn't hurt anyone.

Enjoy wholesome friendships with the many, many people who cross your path. With international travel the big business it is, you'll be surprised at the people who show up in the most unlikely places. And you yourself, as a missionary will travel much more than your counterparts at home. There are trips to and from the mission field, holidays, opportunities for continuing education, conferences in your particular field—many chances to meet new people and renew former acquaintances.

Some of these friendships can grow into love. Perhaps this is in God's plan. Many times this has worked out beautifully: two people from very different parts of their homeland or from two different countries meet in yet a third country. A romance blossoms and leads to marriage.

But there are also situations where things have not worked out so well. This is an area where "slow and steady" is a good motto to observe. If you meet someone in whom you are interested, assuming of course that this person is a believer, and the feeling is shared mutually, pray much and accept good counseling. Go to people on your field. Write home to leaders in your mission, to your home church, to your family. Be very sure before you take a permanent step like marriage. This is especially necessary if the person is from a country other than your own. Even if the person is of the same race and speaks basically the same language, there can be major adjustments that have to be made to bridge the two cultures. For instance I used to get so mad when one of my English friends would want to know, "What time do we feed?" To me, feed is what animals do, not people! Or when I had made a perfectly beautiful apple pie, he wanted to know where the custard sauce was "to wash it down with." These are surmountable obstacles, of course, but don't just jump to the conclusion that just because you are there and he is there, that God has brought you together for anything more than a friendship.

Marrying a national of the country to which you have gone is also a possibility for the single woman missionary. Some of the men are very charming. Some have lived in Britain or America; they seem very Westernized but underneath the sophisticated veneer generally there is a strong nationalistic pull which would require you to give up your ways and accept his. Again, sometimes it works out well. Other times the problems of living in two cultures outweighs the joys of marriage.

In any case, marrying anyone outside of your own particular mission area usually means leaving the mission and your field of service. Be very sure this is what you want. More than that, be sure it is what God wants for you. Especially after a term or more of service, the decision to leave your field is a very serious one. In all likelihood, it means never seeing your adopted land again; never again speaking the language you've struggled so hard to learn; never eating the food you've come to appreciate and crave when you are away from it even for a short while; no longer have part in decision-making concerning cherished projects; losing contact with nationals you may have led to the Lord or nurtured along.

On the opposite side, it means trying to fit back into what is often described as the American "rat-race." Your years overseas will have changed you, possibly in ways imperceptible to you, but obvious to others. After living in the midst of poverty, the waste that is commonplace in the States, is shocking. In Bangladesh I have seen people genuinely grateful for the slip of used soap from a motel room; in America kids leave the cake of soap in the full tub to melt away down the drain. Even that full tub shakes you up after having to heat and carry water to get a quarter of an inch in your tin wash tub.

The topics which occupy people's minds often appear trivial also: Knowing people who may be facing starvation on one side of the world remains prominent in your mind while you are trying to be polite with people who are agonizing over the latest diet fad, or rapturous over their new draperies.

The issues which cause church fights and splits also appear shallow and petty. After hearing a man hold the one edition in his native language and say, "All my life I have wanted a copy of this book," the question of which version of the Bible ought to be used seems preposterous.

The decision to leave your field involves so much—no decision to marry ever ought to be taken lightly, but when it involves leaving a fruitful ministry, the choice is that much harder to make. There is the added burden that much of what was your whole life for however many years you were on the field, will have to stay bottled up inside of you. People quickly tire of hearing about "what we used to do back in . . ."

With the right man, at the right time, the hurdles can be overcome and the former missionary can have a happy and fulfilling life and ministry in the homeland building upon the experiences she lived through on her field. We have seen this happen to one of the first nurses who came to work in our hospital, Jean Weld, or as the nationals still affectionately remember her, *"Lal Chul,"* the redhead. She once told me that she prayed God would keep her committed to her work and the people she lived with, yet flexible enough to marry if that was in God's plans. As it turned out, that was God's plan for Jean. After two very profitable terms in East Pakistan, God led her to her present life as a pastor's wife. When God unfolds His time and His will, it can be beautiful. But marriage ought not to be an escape hatch from a lonely or difficult situation on the mission field.

But let's not be negative. When marriage is in God's plan and left to Him to work out, those out-workings can read like a novel. We know: it happened here in Bangladesh to Karen Carder and Sam Logan.

I first met Sam in the living room of my home in Pasadena, California. I had heard about him before. Billed as a "brilliant young scientist" he was a frequent speaker at conferences and rallies dealing with the subject of Science and the Bible. The billing was not inaccurate. Graduated from Caltech with a Ph.D. in Aeronautics and Astronautics at the age of 25, he was now studying medicine at U.C.L.A. But Sam hadn't come to discuss medicine or science or the Bible. He was about to make his first trip to Asia and wanted all the information he could get. So, sprawled out on the shag carpet he watched my slides and asked questions.

Sam had applied and been accepted for an overseas short term work/study program during his fourth year in medical school. His first choice was the Memorial Christian Hosptial in Malumghat, Bangladesh, but as often happens, the application was lost in the mail and Sam never heard from Malumghat. Instead, he was heading for the Conservative Baptist Hospital in Kalimantan Barat (formerly Borneo).

As pictures of Bangladesh flashed on the make-shift screen, I suggested, "Why not stop by and see Malumghat before you go on to your assignment? When you're traveling that far anyway a few more miles don't make a lot of difference in your total mileage allotment, and who knows if you will ever get back that way again?" The idea made sense. Sam knew Dr. Viggo Olsen who had been the prime mover in establishing the hospital. Sam had followed the hospital's progress and this would be a chance to see it in action. I returned to Bangladesh with a memo about his flight plans and which plane to meet when he arrived in Chittagong.

I met Sam the next time in the living room of my house in Chittagong, Bangladesh. Some of us had gone out to the airport to meet him at the scheduled time, but he wasn't on the plane. We had barely arrived home, however, when in he walked. His flight had been changed, but armed with the sketchy map I had drawn in California, he found us.

He was expected at our hospital (a sixty mile, three hour, bumpy ride away) but they were in the midst of an infectious hepatitis siege. Before he could go to Malumghat, he would have to have a gamma globulin shot. So my "Welcome to Bangladesh, Sam" was with two 5-cc syringes.

We showed him the sights of Chittagong town and sent him on his way the next day. As he was leaving he asked if we knew a lady doctor named Karin Ahlin. She was working in Bangladesh with another mission and he had been asked to look her up. I assured him I knew her and would have her address for him when he returned from Malumghat. Then I added rather glibly, "But if it's Karens you are looking for, we have a nice one at Malumghat."

Karen Carder, an R.N., first came to Bangladesh in January 1973. She accompanied friends from her church to get a taste of life on the mission field with a view to future involvement. I'll let Karen tell you the story—

On arrival in Bangladesh I was hit with nearly overwhelming culture shock: people, transportation, filth, poverty and a general lack of comfort. A state of exhaustion from non-stop traveling certainly intensified the "awfulness." We were immediately taken to Kaptai, the place where the missionaries' Spiritual Life Conference was being held. My pastor was to be the speaker at the conference. Kaptai had been described to me as a resort. You can imagine what my Western mind was thinking! It was like a bad joke. But since no one else seemed to mind the appalling conditions, I felt very much alone in my distress.

At the opening meeting of the Conference, the congregation sang the familiar hymn, "The Lily of the Valley" and the Lord spoke to me through those words,

In sorrow He's my comfort, in trouble He's my stay
He tells me every care on Him to roll . . .
He all my griefs has taken, and all my sorrows borne
In temptation He's my strong and might tower.
I have all for Him forsaken and all my idols torn
From my heart and now He keeps me by His power
He will never, never leave me, not yet forsake me here
While I live by faith and do His blessed will.
A wall of fire about me, I've nothing now to fear
With His manna He my hungry soul shall fill.

Everyone made his way back to his quarters after the service. Ironically, the single girls were staying in what was dubbed the "Honeymoon Cottage". After a gab session, everyone eventually went to sleep. I, however, stayed up nearly all night, while the Lord dealt with the inner rooms of my heart, with those things that were keeping me from service to Him in Bangladesh. The particular areas were cleanliness, the Western way of life, having to leave the American culture and comfortable surroundings. Although I had previously dedicated my life to the Lord, that night marked a new love for the Lord and a desire to serve Him wherever He would choose.

Mark 12:29-31 became *my* verses that night: *"The Lord our God is One Lord* (He will not tolerate idols in our lives). *And thou shalt love the Lord thy God with all thy heart, and with all thy soul and with all thy strength, This is the first commandment. And the second is like it, namely this: Thou shalt love thy neighbor as thyself."*

After that night, the Lord truly had my heart, all of it. He had my love and I knew that He would give me a love for Bangladesh and her people.

By August 1974, Karen was at Malumghat engrossed in Bengali language study. She was contented and happy in her life and looking forward to plunging full time into the hospital's medical/surgical evangelistic program.

Sam arrived at Malumghat on a Tuesday afternoon just as the weekly medical committee meeting was finishing. Since that was the one time when the American medical staff would all be together he was taken directly to the living room of the house where the nurses and school teachers live. Sam was introduced all around and was trying to place everyone, when he saw one more American girl through the curtains and the grill work between the living room and the verandah. Karen had fallen victim to the hepatitis and was not yet well enough to attend the meeting. As she heard sounds of the meeting breaking up, she went out to the living room to have a word with her doctor. In those few minutes Sam and Karen had their first glimpses of each other. Almost immediately, Sam was whisked off to dinner and Karen returned to her room.

Many matchmakers had had their hooks into Sam, suggesting this girl or that one as God's choice for him. But Sam held them at bay by replying, "When I find the right girl, I'll know it." That Tuesday afternoon Sam knew it! He had found Karen. But he only had five days and ostensibly he had come to see the working of the hospital.

Sam enquired of his host and hostess if it were permissible to visit patients with hepatitis. (They innocently assumed he wished to see Dr. Olsen's wife Joan who also had the disease. He made the courtesy call but then had to explain that Joan was not the patient he'd had in mind.) Eventually arrangements were made for Sam to meet Karen, but the time got mixed up and Sam walked in the wrong door, thereby catching Karen in her housecoat at the ironing board. As word of growing interest spread through the mission compound everyone became very helpful—too helpful! Missionary kids suddenly had urgent business which kept them going back and forth in front of the verandah of the nurse's home.

In spite of, or perhaps because of, well meaning missionary friends, kids, cultural taboos, they did find time to be together. They talked and found common interests and mutal aspirations. Not many of us knew that they had come to an "understanding" during those five days, although we were amused that it was decided Sam needed another gamma globulin shot before he left, due to his exposure to hepatitis while at Malumghat! They wrote voluminously during his time in Indonesia and by then none of us was surprised when Karen announced she would be returning to the USA to marry Sam Logan.

They returned to Bangladesh to fill a much needed post when the quota of doctors was short at Malumghat. Now, with Samuel Jr. who joined them in August 1979, they look to the Lord to lead them in their future service as He led them together in the past.

If marriage is in God's plan for you, God will work out the details. You don't have to scheme and finagle.

But this chapter wasn't really meant to be about marriage. The point of this section is friendship for friendship's sake alone, not for any possible deeper relationships in the future.

There are few, if any, places in the world where a person would be forced to remain friendless and alone. Most people are inherently friendly and will respond to warmth as a flower opens to the sun. If being friendly does not come naturally to you, work on it. Start with as simple a gesture as a smile, or a greeting, then move forward from there. Invite people to your home. Schedule times for relaxing, for talking, for recreation. Accept invitations that come your way. Put yourself out in order to be helpful to others. And when you are blessed with friends, cultivate, nurture and cherish them.

[1]Isobel Kuhn, *Ascent to the Tribes* (Chicago: Moody Press, 1956), pages 36-37.

Chapter Five
Assuming You Are the Only One Who Is Busy

Kipling wrote it, "East is east and west is west, and never the twain shall meet."

He was never more correct than in the matter of work, schedules, busyness.

To a person from the East, a mark of spirituality is a calm and quiet way of life. A spiritual man knows how to wait, indefinitely if need be. He doesn't run in all directions like a rubber band ready to snap. The Western concept of rush-rush-rush, work-work-work repels most Asians.

Often before important decisions are to be made, the Asian will spend time—a day or two or more—just sitting. He may be thinking, praying or meditating. To the Westerner, anything more than a reasonable prayer session would be considered a "waste of time." To one from an Eastern culture, however, this quiet time is necessary to eliminate extraneous thoughts, to focus his whole attention on the matter at hand in order to maintain harmony with the people involved.

This area of time and the differences in approach between the Westerner and the Easterner is one of the hardest problems to handle. What to the Easterner is soul-nourishing calm, comes across to the Westerner as laziness. Perhaps Rudyard Kipling summed it up best in his classic:

"Now it is not wise for the Christian's health
To hustle the Aryan brown
For the Christian riles
And the Aryan smiles

And it weareth the Christian down
And the end of it all is a tombstone white
With the name of the late deceased
And an epitath drear: A fool lies here
Who tried to hustle the East."[1]

It is not only in dealing with nationals that problems of busyness arise. It can likewise create tremendous problems between colleagues.

We all get so wrapped up in our work. We all feel we have so much to do. We get that "chicken-with-its-head-cut-off" look about us as we breathlessly gasp, "I'll never get it all done."

Frequently I catch myself working up to a full blown case of "busyitis." In those times I have been helped by repeating, almost as a prayer, the words from John Greenleaf Whittier's poem:

Drop Thy still dews of quietness
Till all our strivings cease
Take from our souls the strain and stress
And let our ordered lives confess
The beauty of Thy peace.

Many times problems with our colleagues arise because so often we tend to feel that no one else can possible have as much to do as I do. Nobody else can possibly be as busy as I am.

Busyness is a state of mind often having little or nothing to do with work responsibilities. It is very possible to be busy doing nothing! Actually it is highly possible for a missionary to be very lazy. There are no time clocks to punch. The missionary is generally able to set his own schedule. Sometimes the day which loomed so full of possibilities gets frittered away by time-consuming trivia. In many locations each unit of work is a law unto itself—no one is responsible to check what is going on. Often there are no concerned pastors (or ones brave enough) either on the field or during furlough to ask why you didn't attend the special prayer meeting or engage in a particular outreach. Yes, there are prayer letters and reports to supporters, but these can be fudged or shrouded in what Dr. Donald McGavran called "foggy words" such as "The Lord is really blessing." A statement like that doesn't tell if there has been a revival in the church, or if there is a new baby in the family, or if the chickens are laying.

In recent years, more and more churches are asking, "Who collects the report cards for the missionaries?" Some churches send periodic questionnaires to the people they support, but often these are lacking in focus. Rather than being concerned about work loads, goals, problems in priority decision making, they ask spiritualized questions: "How many souls did you lead to the Lord last month?" not realizing that preparing the soil, planting the seed, nurturing the new plants—these are the difficult time consuming tasks. Or the questionnaire reflects the current theological debate in America. We've been through Day/Age versus Gap theory, four or five point Calvinism, Co-operative Evangelism, fund raising as opposed to living by faith, etc. etc. ad infinitum. Each of these may come with the veiled threat of support being dropped if you don't adhere to the particular point of view of the people who prepared the questions.

Such questionnaires don't help the missionary in setting personal and work objectives and priorities. Rather, they add to the rationalization: "I can't get anything done around here for all the paper work I have to do."

Now it may be I've alienated you and made you about ready to throw this book away because of my suggestion that you or any of the missionaries you know, are lazy! Why, you work from dawn to dark! You barely have enough time to greet your family or housemates, certainly not enough to work in your garden, or read a book or have some fun.

Your complaint may be quite legitimate, and I apologize for including you with the others who might not be as diligent, but I also wonder about all that activity. Office jobs, hospital duty, teaching positions: I wonder if that is what the missionary's job is all about in these days. We are living in a different era from when modern missions began. A new age calls for new approaches. Most countries of the world, especially the so-called emerging countries, are strongly nationalistic. They want the job opportunities, including the top positions, for their own people, not for a series of expatriates who rotate the posts among themselves. The most important work a missionary can do is to train somebody else to do his job. In this age just about everything else ought to be stripped in order to allow missionaries to teach nationals, especially those in positions of leadership. The Lord Jesus knew the importance of this. He selected a few men and trained them so that

—"They should be with Him and
—that they should go forth to preach."

Rather than everyone's being caught up in routine tasks, whether medical or ministerial, the work would be farther ahead if "each one were to teach one," as Dr. Frank Laubach coined the phrase. The Scripture gives the pattern in II Timothy 2:2. This carries it one step further than just your teaching another person. It implies that you teach people of such a calibre that they in turn can teach others.

No matter what professional label you wear, no matter what appears on your job description, you need to take the time to be involved in working closely with nationals. Everyone ought to be discipling someone else. Everyone ought to be working himself out of a job. The president of my mission, Dr. Wendell Kempton, quoted a statement which has burned its way into my heart more and more fervently as I see how God has worked in the literature ministry in which I am involved, and has caused it to grow beyond my wildest imagination. He said,

"Success without a successor is failure."

So often we find it simpler to do the job ourselves rather than show someone else how to do it. Perhaps it is just a bit humbling that someone else might be able to do it as well as we do or even better. Perhaps we are afraid to allow innovations and unusual methods. But if we are to build anything of lasting value, we must let other people get into our shoes. They must make their mistakes—as we have. They must be encouraged to try.

But all this encouraging, training, discipling takes time. And that is just what we feel we don't have. The key here is organization. Getting things planned so that you are able to do a number of things in one day. Volumes have been written on how to become organized. Some people make out a list the day before and enjoy striking off each item. Some people become frustrated by seeing the long list of items still undone.

And others faithfully make out the list—but lose it before they get started. There are daily planners, notebooks, all sorts of methods and tools to help you in your strategy and day by day functioning. Find the method that works for you.

In recent years I have read many books on the management of time, as I am sure you have. One list of 15 ways to be more productive left me so discouraged I was ready to give up even trying. That list contained pointers such as:

—Use your spare time to get several things done at once.
—Crack the whip over yourself. Require production of yourself.
—Start vigorously and promptly each morning.
—Make yourself work. Don't let your moods control your work.

I was tired out before I had even finished reading the 15 points!
Then at a Spiritual Life Conference where the theme was *"In
quietness and confidence shall be your strength,"* (Isaiah 30:15) a
group of us began discussing how we could cut down on the frenzy
and really do things which were of lasting value. Several months later,
we invited Dr. Russell Ebersole, former missionary to the Philippines
and now an executive in our mission, to lead a session on time management. The Biblical principles he gave us that evening are among the
finest I have read or heard. I present them here for you:

The Lord's Use of Time—as Applied to His Servants
1. Our Lord was very conscious that His Father had a plan for His
    life. John 5:30; John 6:38; Hebrews 10:7; John 17:4
    Are you sure that you are in the center of God's will for you TO-
    DAY?
2. To Our Lord, it was imperative that He follow the Father's will.
    John 9:4; John 4:34. We too have only a limited amount of time
    in which to do the Father's will. Will we be able to say like Paul,
    "I have finished my course?"
3. Our Lord knew that there was adequate time to fulfill the Father's
    will in His life. He often spoke of "my hour"—that didn't just
    apply to climatic experiences but to every hour of His life. John
    2:4; 7:3; John 8:20; 12:23; 12:22; 13:1; 17:1

    Our lives are often a list of unfinished tasks, unwritten letters, un-
    read books, etc. Yet as Amy Carmichael wrote, "There are
    enough hours in every day to do God's will for us in that day."
    Every week has 168 hours in it. Let's look at a possible schedule:
        56 hours for sleep and relaxation
        21 hours for meals
        56 hours for main occupation, job, study, etc.
        ———
        133 hours accounted for

    That leaves 35 hours or 5 hours a day. How do we spend those:
    Oswald Sanders said, "The use of time depends largely on the
    pressure of motives."
4. Our Lord lived an ordered life. Even though He had many re-
    sponsibilities, He was not pressured by emergencies and crises.
    We need to be careful not to let the urgent crowd out the really

important. General Dwight D. Eisenhower said, "Urgent matters are seldom important; Important matters are seldom urgent."

There is a barrenness in an overly busy life. Learn to reverse the work ethic maxim so that it reads, "Don't do today what *can* be put off until tomorrow." In the interval it might become clear that it need not be done at all.

Consider Jesus' actions in John 11:6. He didn't rush away from what He was doing at the time, because He knew what He would do later would be better for all concerned.

5. Our Lord had time for people. His was not an attitude of, "Come back some other time, I'm busy now." Mark 10:13; Mark 5:35; Philippians 2:20.

It takes time to get to know people. You must be with a person in order to know him. Don't consider the people who break into your busy schedule as a bother or an irritation. Interruptions did not disturb the Lord's peace because He knew that those too had been planned for in God's schedule for that day. Rather than being upset by those who throw your plans out of line, thank God that people come to see you. That's the whole purpose behind serving the Lord and others. Allow time for interruptions: for that knock on the door from someone who needs you, and especially for the little voice that says, "Mommy, Daddy, read me a story."

6. Our Lord put first things first. He had His priorities straight. In Mark 1:35-38 we read, *"All men seek Thee."* But Jesus said, *"Let us go into the next town."* Jesus didn't get sidetracked from God's will by the multitudes. What are our priorities in life and ministry? Are we doing everything to see that these are being carried out? Paul said, *"This ONE thing I do . . ."* There are a lot of people doing a lot of things halfway, but few doing one thing really well. Ask yourself:

    —What am I doing now that really doesn't need to be done? We can be extremely busy doing things God never intended us to do at all.

    —What am I doing now that really could/should be done by someone else? We need to learn to delegate jobs. It is a fact we spend our time doing those things we enjoy doing, or that we may be good at doing, although these may not be top priority items.

    —Is what I am doing part of a larger task or goal to which I am committed?

    —Is this the best way to do this?

—Is what I am doing wasting my or another person's time?

7. Our Lord took time to be alone with His Father. One of the reasons we are doing what we should not be doing, and not doing what we should be doing, is because we don't take the time to find out what God has planned. We don't spend the time to listen to Him. (Psalm 46:10; Mark 6:31; Mark 3:13; Luke 10:41; Philippians 3:13; Isaiah 30:15.)

Dr. Ebersole's point seven hits the nail on the head. The problem of busyness, the problem of living in harmony with others can be solved only when a person makes the effort to spend time with his Heavenly Father. There will be those who feel it should not be necessary to write such words to missionaries and prospective missionaries. I know first hand the difficulties of establishing and maintaining a regular program of Bible study and prayer. I can think of more things that simply *have* to be done during the time I've set aside for devotions. For a while I used to fool myself by saying, "Lord, I'm really more of the do-er type. Let me work while somebody else sits and prays, okay?" Then I read, really read the great missionary verse:

"Pray ye therefore the Lord of the harvest that He would sent forth laborers into His harvest." (Luke 10:2).

To whom was the Lord speaking in that verse? To the seventy disciples. To the very people He was sending out to preach and teach and heal. The missionaries themselves must be pray-ers as well as do-ers.

The person who has spent time with the Lord, getting his day planned will be more ready to meet the day.

The spiritual side, however, is not in isolation from the practical life. Sometimes a reminder of simple courtesy and common sense is in order.

To the *married:* Don't assume that because a person is unmarried, he or she will have more time available. That is not generally true. In addition to the hours spent at regular tasks in a hospital, school, office visitation program, etc. the unmarried person still has to manage the house, arrange for meals, entertain company, take care of clothes, prepare lessons, tend to correspondence. Most of these are ordinary, everyday things that have to be done whether a person is married or single. In a family, often the everyday tasks can be shared, dividing the load among more people, whereas the single person might have to handle them all alone. Don't pile a lot of work on the singles because you assume "they have nothing else to do anyway."

To the *unmarried:* Be patient with your married sisters. When they don't come to work, or they don't get the lesson written on time, or don't finish the report you need, or can't come to teach the class— consider that maybe they were up all night with a sick baby. Perhaps an older child needed them at home. Remember the priorities here. She is not responsible to you. She's responsible first to God, then to her husband; anything else she may be doing comes further down the line.

Sometimes people who aren't married accuse the wives of doing nothing but keeping house. The question is raised, "What did they come to the mission field for? They could have stayed home and done what they do here." Sometimes the unmarried forget the married women's home is top priority. That home can be so important in a heathen culture. How will national believers learn to raise their children for Christ unless they see a model?

But, back to the *married women:* don't allow your home to totally detract you from active participation in the ministry to which the Lord called you. The very fact that homemaking is *top* priority indicates there are other priorities as well which must be worked into your schedule. Don't decide that keeping house is the sum total of what you will do on the mission field. Don't use your husband and children as an excuse not to learn the language or not to do any missionary work at all.

The matter of stewardship of her time is one which is difficult for the married woman. Among mission organizations there is a difference of opinion. In some missions, every person is a missionary in his or her own right, whether married or not. In other organizations, a married woman is a missionary's wife, and is not expected to participate in the overall program of missionary work. A couple would do well to understand this difference even before choosing the mission board under which they will serve.

Some married women feel that what is required of them is that they be "keepers of the home"; good wives and mothers. Certainly this is a biblical priority. For the Christian wife that important job is covered in the verse where Jesus said, *"these ye ought to have done."* (Matthew 23:33).

But being a good wife and mother is a biblical requirement for all Christian wives. For those who have chosen to be missionary wives and mothers that is just step one. There are further requirements for you. These will vary with your own training and the ages of your children. Often the complaint has been raised by people visiting the mission fields that wives do less than they would be doing at home. Your contemporaries back home often are holding down a full eight hour a day job. Perhaps some work outside of the home to better their careers when they would do well to stay at home, but in these days many must work in order to keep the family solvent. Yet those women come home from a day's work, do the shopping, cooking, housework. They are also Sunday School teachers, youth group leaders, serve on committees, sing in the choir, etc. They are also the ones who are sending money so that you can stay on the mission field. In effect they are paying your salary.

Missionary service requires more of you than it does of those in the homelands in terms of spiritual service, or in the many facets involved in the smooth running of a mission overseas. It requires more because you have chosen to be a "Second Decision" Christian.

The Old Testament talks in detail about Second Decision people. These are those who have decided to serve God at any cost. The Old Testament example is the basis for the books of Ezra, Nehemiah, Haggai and Zechariah.

You know the story: because of their idolatry and repeated ignoring of God's commandments, the people of Israel were sent into captivity in Babylon. They lived there under the reigns of various kings: Ahasuerus, Nebuchadnezzar, Belshazzar, Darius, and then Cyrus. Cyrus was unique in the ancient world in his respect for the gods, customs and rulers of the people he subjugated. Some Jews saw him as a God-sent deliverer, but many failed to respond to his encouragement to leave Babylon and to reestablish the religious, and political life of Israel. Josephus said, "they were unwilling to leave their possessions." Many of God's people were content just to know Him, but not to be part of His plan. Only 4200 Jews made the journey back through the desert to establish the milieu into which Christ could be born. Those 4200 people are "Second Decision" people. The first decision is that of belonging to God at all; the second is that of being part of His program and plan.

In this day there is a similar situation. How many millions claim to belong to Christ—first decision! Statistics prove how few are willing to follow Him completely no matter where that may lead—the second decision! The Apostle Paul in writing to *believers* gave the admonition, *"Present your bodies a living sacrifice"* (Romans 12:1).

It is not that these Second Decision people are some kind of super-saints. Far from it. The remnant of Jews who returned from Babylon fell prey to nearly every attack of Satan. Missiologist Dr. Arthur Glasser gives seven separate problems which were resolved through the ministry of the prophets after the Jews' return from exile. He lists these as major problems, relevant for missionaries *today:*

1. When spiritual life is dull and barren with little evidence of God's blessing, the problem may be the loss of priorities (generally through selfishness)—Haggai 1:1-15.
2. When discouragement overtakes the servants of God, the problem may be their lack of faith (generally through an unwarranted self-confidence)—Haggai 2:1-9.
3. When anticipated blessings are unmistakably withheld, the problem may arise from the neglect of worship (generally through sloth or excessive activism)—Haggai 2:10-19; Zechariah 1:1-6.
4. When the people of God find their enemies growing bold and their fears multiplying, the problem may arise from their superficial regard for God and their indifference toward cultivating him— Haggai 2:20-23.
5. When the work in which one is engaged appears to languish, this may be due to the lack of vision of local leadership—Zechariah 1:7-2:13.
6. When workers are tempted to quit, this may be due to their preoccupation with morbid introspection and self-depreciation and their failure to distinguish the scolding of the enemy from the conviction of the Spirit—Zechariah 3:1-10.
7. When leaders fail to lead and their followers lose both their concord and buoyance, the problem may have arisen from neglecting the Holy Spirit—Zechariah 4:1-14.

No, those second decision people were not perfect, nor are those today who decide to choose God in "full-time service." But it is because of their having made that decision that God requires more of them.

It is a matter of priorities. There may be some things that you just won't have time to do around the house, but I've observed that the kids remember going out visiting with Mommy to play the Gospel Recordings records, much more than whether the gingerbread cookies were iced or not. They are going to look back on the times when the whole family folded the leaflets advertising the special meetings much more than whether the bedroom was always spic and span.

Encourage the children to have a part in the work. When I was a child my father was successively the Canadian director of two different leprosy missions. The office was short-staffed and often my brother and I were conscripted to fold letters, stuff envelopes, lick stamps. I don't remember it's being any hardship. Rather we felt we were needed to keep the whole ministry going ahead. One of those was very much a "Faith Mission" (Whose faith? Sometimes I was not sure.) What donations came in went first to the mission projects, then if any was left over, we got it. You can be sure, the highlight of our day was finding the answer to the question "What came in the mail?"—an engrossment that has not left me to this day.

Some women feel they must make everything exactly as it would have been back home, or they are robbing their family of its heritage. In actual fact most children who have grown up on the mission field have a far greater hankering for the national dishes than they do for Grandma's apple pie. There may be some traditions that you would have kept up had you stayed at home, but you didn't stay there. You are among those who have heard God's second call—a call to serve Him in a foreign land.

Sometimes keeping up all the traditions from home is a form of culture shock. It is a security blanket to prepare the same delicacies you had in your home as a child. I'm not knocking pumpkin pie and Christmas cookies. I am just saying that if the necessity to have those things becomes more important than entering into service for the Lord, then perhaps there needs to be an adjustment of priorities.

Don't slave to preserve everthing exactly as it would have been had you never left Hometown, USA. A contemporary wall plaque puts it succinctly,

"There is no point in doing well what ought not be be done at all."

Learn to be innovative rather than relying on the traditional. I confess I am a traditionalist at heart. I like things to be as they have been "world without end." But there is no use in frustrating yourself and others if things can't be done exactly as they were back home.

Experiment with local fruits and vegetables. You and your kids may come to like them—at least as well as they like vegetables in any part of the world! We have a long, green, soft, rather tasteless, innocuous vegetable that graces our tables from May to November every year. We call it "chichinga"—that sounds more appealing to me than snake gourd which I understand is its English name. But whatever the adults may think of it, ten-year-old Doug, upon learning it wasn't an every-day dish in the States said, "Mom, don't they have chichinga in America. Could we take a barrel of it home with us?"

Some people feel that to maintain proper health they must have imported food or meals identical to what they ate in their homeland.

That isn't true. You can study your local products and learn to substitute: guavas for apples, pumpkin for your yellow vegetable when there are no carrots, etc.

Establishing a truly Christian home, raising children to know and serve the Lord: those are basic requirements for all parents. Over and above that, missionary parents both must have a clear conscience that they are spending their time in a responsible way before those to whom they are accountable—their supporters, their mission board, their God.

As with so many other things, people likewise tend to go to two extremes in their work situations.

On the one hand, some, who while they may fill their days with busyness, in actual fact accomplish very little. A missionary home on furlough from Ethiopia shared with me a devotional given by a national pastor which illustrates this point. The message was from I Kings, chapter 20. Boastful King Ben-Hadad sent insulting threats to Israel's King Ahab. For once Ahab was smart enough to listen to the prophet of the Lord. The prophet told of having been commissioned to guard a captive, but *"While your servant was busy here and there, the man disappeared."*

So often as Christian workers, we are busy "here and there", busy with this and that and we miss carrying out the commission given to us by the Lord.

On the other hand, other people put out tremendous volumes of work, but work is their whole life. They can be termed workaholics, never or at least seldom taking time off for relaxation and reflection.

Since I have the tendency to fall into this latter category, I am indebted to my own mother for the insights gained in the following devotional, written especially for homemakers, but applicable to all.

In our day there is much emphasis on leisure time.

However, for so many of us who were brought up in the Puritan work ethic mold, it's difficult to accept time for ourselves. We have to remind ourselves that it's not necessarily a cardinal virtue to work from dawn till dark.

We can learn from the Arab who just sat down one day—when he was asked what he was doing, his reply was, "I'm letting my soul catch up with my body." We need times to do nothing. We all return to our duties much the better for having had some time off. The chance to walk away from pressure for even a short time helps us to gain a fresh perspective. It can restore our calm and revitalize us to be more effective.

The length of the free time is not so important as the fact of it. It's something to look forward to, to break the monotomy or alleviate the grind. And it's important that *we feel no guilt*—no "policeman over our shoulder" sense of wrongdoing for having taken a break.

The Bible speaks of "pleasures for evermore" in the future (Psalm 16:11). We can feel sure that the Lord is not against either leisure or pleasure in moderation while we are here on earth.[2]

[1]Rudyard Kipling, "The Naulakha" from *Songs From the Book* (New York Doubleday, Doran and Co., 1920), page 110.

[2]Jeannette Lockerbie, *More Salt in My Kitchen* (Chicago: Moody Press, 1980), pages 63, 64.

Chapter Six

Dependance and Independance

In many people's minds independence means the ability to be a jack-of-all-trades.

I hang my head in shame because there are an awful lot of things I just can't do. That recruit who had to move the box for me at Candidate School had probably run into inept types like me who can't get the key to turn in the lock, or contend with foldback car seats, or any of a hundred daily situations others cope with, seemingly with utmost ease. Having so said, here goes—

To *unmarried women:* try first to do it yourself, or ask another woman to help. Many are very capable. They know how to change fuses and check the oil in the engine and change the wick in the kerosene lantern. There is nothing unfeminine about knowing how to handle or even enjoy doing those things. When you or your colleagues can't manage, however, don't be too proud to ask a man to help.

When a missionary man does come over to make a repair or adjust some mechanical monster, be thankful for his brotherly concern. It may be that the same thing is broken back at his home and he hasn't quite found a moment to fix it, but he feels a certain responsibility to come and help a fellow worker who may have no one there to help her. Accept his help graciously but don't abuse this concern by calling him unnecessarily.

The converse of learning to do things yourself is allowing a man to be a gentleman. We are losing some of these values in these days of equality among the sexes, but I'd venture to say, most women still enjoy having a man open the doors, carry the packages, seat them at the table and generally just be a gentleman. Accept this gracefully and in no way cause embarrassment to a man considerate enough to treat you as a lady. During furlough in the States one time, I observed such a scene. A number of us—old friends—were sitting around enjoying an after Sunday dinner chat. One of the women had to leave. It happened that she had some packages, enough to occupy both hands. Courteously the grown-up son of the home jumped up to help her, but she spurned his offer with, "I can do it myself," and brushing him off with her elbows she struggled her way out to her car. I thought, *If that's being independent, Lord deliver me from it!* I can still see the look on the young man's face.

When a colleague goes out of his way to help with something in your house, it is thoughtful to show your appreciation. Perhaps some "goodies" from the kitchen, an invitation to a meal, or a goofy gift. Be very careful, however, to include his wife in these expressions of thanks. Satan would love to twist helpfulness and gratefulness into occasions for jealousy and suspicion. Don't let him.

The *married women,* too, need to be or learn to be self-sufficient. There are likely to be many, many times when your husband will be away preaching or on business. There will undoubtedly be times when you will have to make decisions without his advice. There will be times when you will have to stay alone.

Learn to depend on God for safety, rather than having to have some one with you all the time. One married woman always called her unmarried colleague to come and stay with her when her husband was away, because, "I could never stay alone in the house. I'd be too scared." Yet the unmarried lady routinely lived alone.

Many times your husband will be busy in very important work. Rather than asking him to leave that to help you, you could learn to work that screwdriver and fix the broken "thingamajig." In many countries missionaries have household help. That "convenience" isn't always all it's cracked up to be as when all your laundry turns bright blue from being washed all together, or when the person washing the dishes breaks the handle off the cast iron frying pan which was your grandmother's. Most often, however, the people who help us in our homes are capable of doing things in their own way. There are many items they can get working again or they can arrange for the plumber, electrician or whatever. You don't always have to nag your husband or wait until he is available to do some household chore.

For example, we needed a particular trunk one day, but it was stacked in the storage area up over the kitchen ironically called a "go-down" in this part of the world. First we were told by the wife in the family that we couldn't have the box until her husband returned and was able to get it down. Later in the day she called in another missionary man to crawl up and get it. Yet all the time in her house there were perfectly able national helpers who could have managed the small problem quite well. Learn to use the resources around you to good advantage.

Don't *stop* doing on the mission field what you were perfectly able to to do at home. For instance a group of new missionaries arrived on our field and I was collecting driver's licenses to turn in to the motor vehicle department. One husband piped up, "My wife won't be driving here." That seemed utter nonsense to me. Be sure you do learn to drive. Your life or the life of your children might at some time depend upon your being able and willing to drive. This applies equally if you are in a boat or plane ministry. Learn how to run that engine. It is not unladylike to get your hands dirty and to know how to make things function.

Learn to be competent in areas where it is necessary—perhaps for survival. The "clinging vine" woman is going out of style in the time we are living in. And none of you who are involved in or are considering serving in a foreign mission assignment are that type of woman anyway. We all know of families where the husband says, "Let's go serve the Lord on the mission field." The wife envisioning cannibals and snakes and sickness says, "No way!" and that's the end of that. But you aren't that sort of person or you wouldn't likely be deliberately reading this book. You have enough trust in God and adventure in your soul to at least consider a cross-cultural mission. You *can* learn to do things. Do learn, that will save much time and frustration.

For parents and teachers, the concept of learning to do things yourself carries one step further into teaching children to do things. Sometimes harrassed mothers complain, "There is so much work to do around here. I can't possibly get it all done." And all the time, they have two, three or more helpers. Potential helpers, that is! For they must be taught, motivated, stimulated, encouraged or, in extreme cases, *made* to carry their load of the work around the house.

On mission fields where it is necessary to have cooks, sweepers, bearers, ayahs, it makes it doubly hard to train children to fulfill their duties at home.

For a few weeks when I was eight or nine, we kept a family of missionaries who were home on furlough from India. While the mother was undergoing medical tests, the father and three children lived with us. Mealtimes were a horror with one after the other of the children

demanding service: "Get me some water," "I need a towel, I've spill-
ed the soup." "Take away this plate." And so on. Their father dis-
missed all of this by explaining they were used to having servants surrounding the table to meet their needs. To which my mother replied,
(after days and days of such provocation) "I am not your servant.
There is the kitchen. You may get yourself a drink of water. And now
you may help me clear the table."

How much better for a child to learn in his own home, whether that
be in America or Angola. Working together as a family around the
house can be made into a fun time. Saturday morning was "clean up
the house" time in my home as a child. No one went anywhere or became involved in activities of his own until the house was ready for the
Lord's Day and the guests who inevitably would arrive. (Dad, of
course, was in his study at the church.) Sometimes we played games as
we worked, or sang, or listened to music or the radio. Everyone was
involved, then everyone was free to go about his own business.

Picking up toys, putting away clothes, setting the table—so many
things even tiny children enjoy doing "just like the grown-ups". As
children mature, they can be expected to be responsible for certain
household duties: cleaning their own room, preparing a particular
meal each week, folding and putting away the clean clothes. The list
will vary with the circumstances and the ages of the children, but no
child—boy or girl—should miss out on the obligations and the joys of
housekeeping just because there are servants in the house. Learn to do
things yourself, then pass on your knowledge to the children.

Among the early missionaries on our field was a couple, both of
whom were doctors. The mother had grown up on a mission field herself and attended boarding school from the time she was six. She felt
she had missed out on a lot in not learning to cook and keep house, so
she began sending her seven year old daughter to my house to learn to
bake brownies and cookies. We had great fun in the making and the
eating, and soon were joined by a two-year younger brother who said,
"I want to learn, too."

Please notice the choice of words throughout this chapter. It talks
of being competent, capable, learning to do things. It does not say
"learn to be independent". An independent missionary is a contradic-
tion of terms, for the Bible says in I Corinthians 3:9, *"We are
labourers together with God."*

I often wince inwardly when a girl, usually to cover up obtuseness
or just plain rudeness, states, "I guess I'm just too independent."

And I may do more than just wince inwardly when the well-meaning visitor impressed by what God has allowed us to do in this particular field pipes up, "You girls are so independent." That is not a compliment. And it is not true.

Dr. W. Wilbert Welch, past president of the Grand Rapids Baptist Seminary writes concerning the matter of independence,

> There are pioneers who are pioneers by nature, calling and gifts; but in general the Scriptures point out the interrelationship of the Spirit's gifts and that we need each other for real strength of impact. There may be occasions when a missionary is a loner because he fears the more sophisticated centers. His independence may be prompted by a spirit which brooks no one opposing his ideas and methods. It could stem from a fear of his labors being too visible to fellow missionaries or even from his having an abrasive, rather brittle spirit which militates against any close relationship so essential to team efforts. It is an inescapable conclusion that Paul was a team man and that gifted men stood with him in nearly every endeavor. The mutual encouragement of their hearts for the labor, the fellowship in prayer, the multiple service gifts of the Spirit complementing each other, the sense of strength stemming from a united effort—all these point to the need of at least considering the team approach.[1]

Rather than being independent, the missionary is entirely dependent. He is:

—dependent upon God
—dependent upon God's people for prayer
—dependent upon his constituency to support him financially
—dependent upon family and friends for encouragement, help, maybe CARE packages from time to time
—dependent upon household help to keep things running smoothly
—dependent upon nationals to carry out and carry on the work

Independence is not something to be sought after. Many emerging nations have learned this to their sorrow. Many thinking people within the third world look back to the days of colonialism with at least mixed feelings. And yet, perhaps a nation, an organization, a church can afford to be independent just because of the sheer weight of numbers pushing toward the same goal. An individual cannot afford that. Everyone needs people. God said, "It is not good that man should be alone."

We don't have to be taught to be independent. That is an inborn trait. The toddler says, "I can do it myself," as he falls and bumps his nose.

I had just written those words when the idea was confirmed for me in my daily reading in the "Walk Thru the Bible" studies on the Prophets,

> Medical Science has yet to discover a hand or an eye or a kidney capable of "going it alone." Each organ needs the other members of the body to sustain it and nourish it. The only truly independent organs are amputated, dead and useless.
>
> The same holds true in the body of Christ. Each member of the body needs the other members for strength, support, encouragement, and edification. There is a divinely established sense of interdependence.[2]

In acquiring the many skills necessary to be effective as Christian workers, the thing we need most to learn—and it is hard to learn—is, interdependence on God and on one another.

[1]W. Wilbert Welch, "The Christian Mission and Fundamentalism"—position paper for Informissions Conference, 1978, page 20.

[2]Reprinted by kind permission of Walk Through The Bible Ministries.

Chapter Seven

Taking Care of Yourself

For a few years when I was asked to sing a solo, I chose the hymn, "Let me burn out for Thee," each line a stirring sentiment of service and devotion for the Lord.

I don't sing that song anymore because I don't really think that is what God wants us to do. God has given us these bodies, these temples where the Holy Spirit dwells. He expects us to treat our bodies with respect and care for them as we would for a precious gift. He does not intend that we kill ourselves—literally that is—by burning the candle at both ends, by pushing forward when we are at the edge of exhaustion, or by straining the body's delicate mechanisms to the breaking point.

So the thrust of this chapter can be stated simply: Take care of yourself. Take care of yourself so God can use you. "Yourself" is what God has to use in the particular place where you are.

First, *Personal Habits:*

Never "let yourself go", no matter where you live—in the jungle, out in a remote village or in some great, big, impersonal city—keep yourself clean, neat, well pressed, tidy.

There are a couple of traps that people fall into. The unmarried may say, "Nobody is going to look at me anyway. It doesn't matter what I look like."

And the married women say, "I got my man! I don't have to worry about how I look now. I can dress however I please."

Don't fall into either of those snares. They're self-defeating. Keep yourself looking as attractive as you possible can.

The question, "What shall I wear?" is probably as old as

womanhood itself. I wonder if Eve had a choice of leaves? For the female servant of the Lord, the criteria for her clothing must be modesty. She should dress in such a way as to be a credit, not a disgrace to the Lord. That does not mean her trademark will be "missionary frump." An outmoded, unattractive outfit can draw just as much attention as the latest extreme style.

I'll never forget coming home on my first furlough. Lynn, Becky and I were traveling together and decided we'd "do" Europe en route to the States. Knowing we'd be spending a few days in London, I wrote ahead to a cousin whom I had not previously met. As first string bass violinist in the London Philharmonic, this man's contacts were more in the artistic line than in the missionary. He wondered how he would know his world traveling cousin and her friends as they disembarked from the plane. At a loss, he consulted people who were also meeting our flight and was given these clues: "Since they're missionaries coming from a tropical, underdeveloped country, they'll likely be wearing long cotton dresses and their hair will be straggly."

What my cousin didn't know was that we had gone on a shopping spree in Rome: new suit, shoes, bag and had visited a beauty parlor in Paris. As I recall I located him in the airport lounge long before he picked us out of the crowd.

No missionary need fit into the frumpy stereotype. Your friends at home can send magazine clippings or patterns showing what's "in" then select from among the choices what you know is right for you. It's a fact: when you look good, you feel good, and when you feel good, you are able to accomplish far more. Take the time to have your hair done—cut, styled, set, permed, whatever is necessary. Spend some time and thought on your wardrobe. Remodel if needed. Coordinate pieces. Experiment for varying effects. Make occasions to dress up. Even if nobody is coming in for the evening, the old-fashioned custom of changing for dinner has merit. A warm bath—or a cool shower, as the case may be—a fresh dress, neatly styled hair, a splash of cologne: these things can lift you out of the doldrums.

The customs of the country in which you are serving the Lord must become well recognized and respected. There have been times when the preaching of the Gospel has been nullified by the costume of the speaker. In some places no "decent" woman would wear slacks; in other places the pant suit was the national dress long before it hit the West. In some places sleeveless dresses are shocking; in others not only the bare arms but six inches of bare midriff are likewise acceptable.

In many instances it will be correct to wear the national dress of the country where you are working. Be sure to wear this properly—even the sari, which is just a piece of cloth six yards long, can be worn in fashion or not. In wearing national dress, it is wise to check out your outfit ahead of time. I remember feeling like a fool at a picnic awhile ago. I knew we were going to be climbing to a waterfall and sticking our feet in the pool and eating with our fingers and sitting on the ground, so I wore my "grubbies". As the group piled onto the bus, I was dazzled by the swish of silk and nylon saris and confronted by women and girls who had put on their best. They were going on an outing. They would have their pictures taken beside the beauty spot. "What if your clothes get soiled or torn?" I asked. The answer was, "Then we will always remember that it was on that lovely picnic it happened."

The saying is, "clothes make the man" but even nice clothes can't hide a body that is not cared for properly.

Eat correctly to maintain good health. Watch your weight—this includes those for whom either overweight or underweight can be a problem. Even if you live alone, cook good, balanced meals and sit down to eat in pleasant surroundings. Squelch the urge to prop up your study materials against the catsup bottle as you gulp down your sandwich.

Especially when eating with a group of people, be sure to use correct table manners. Hearing someone gulping and slurping is enough to spoil anyone's appetite. Be careful about basic points such as taking small bites, not talking with your mouth full, not leaving the spoon in a cup or a bowl when you drink—that's very hard on eyes! The underlying issue is this: don't forget your good breeding just because you are no longer in the place where you learned it.

Get enough rest. Plan times of recreation, relaxation, exercise. If you have no place to play tennis or jog, at least you can jump rope!

Guard against being offensive by unpleasant breath, body odor, dandruffy hair, foot odors. In summary: take care of yourself.

Likewise, don't neglect your house; keep it clean and nice.

Sometimes this is very difficult. There are often a lot of people in and out. The rooms might be small and crowded and have no closet space, or the building might be a museum piece with 14 foot high ceilings and plaster that showers on your head each time it rains. Rather than giving up, accept it as a challenge to your interior decorating skills and see how you score on a Better Homes and Gardens "before and after" set of pictures.

If at all possible take your pretty knick-knacks with you to the mission field or acquire new ones along the way. Those familiar, lovely things can be like a breath of fresh air on a sultry day.

I inherited my love of English bone china from my mother. In each of the many houses we lived in as I was growing up there was always a glass-doored china cabinet, a three cornered what-not or a hutch. There, displayed for all to enjoy were the delicate cups and saucers. But we didn't just look at them, we used them regularly. When helping me pack drums for my first term of service, my mother suggested I choose out some I would like to take along. Thinking practically rather than esthetically I said, "Oh no. They might break. I will have to take plastic dishes."

My mother quietly asked, "And what do you think missionaries used before there was plastic?"

So I have china plates and cups and saucers. Yes, a few have been broken, but so have the plastic ones. The missionary women and the nationals too enjoy the experience of drinking from a china cup. "The tea tastes so much better in the Shelley's Dainty Blue," says one dear friend.

Wherever you live, make that house a home. Every woman is innately a homemaker, although it seems some educating may be necessary along that line. Once a government report required us to list the various occupations represented by our missionaries. We came up with a list of 20 vocations inclucing the one of homemaker. The first name on the list happened to be an older married woman. We started to check off "homemaker" for her but were corrected by a man saying, "She's not a homemaker now, her children are all grown."

Later a man prayed, "May those of us who have homes be a good example to our neighbors." I felt like interrupting the prayer to say, "Hey, wait a minute. We all have homes and we all need to be examples to our neighbors."

A home with little children in it is indeed a blessed place, but it is not less a home when occupied by a childless couple or by the many varied combinations of unmarried women. Why do homes where single people live get stuck with names like hostel, residence, quarters? The place where people live is their HOME and it is up to the inhabitants to cultivate and develop all the heart-warming, cozy atmosphere the word HOME brings to mind.

While vacationing in India, we learned of a single lady, now well along in years. She lived and worked on an isolated station, but she had created there such an atomosphere of peace that other missionaries loved to spend a few days of "R&R" with her and bask in her homey influence.

Keep yourself stimulated mentally.

We all like to talk about our work and share what we are doing. But don't fall into the trap of being able to talk *only* about the work. It must be upsetting and even a bit disgusting to the non-medically oriented person to have ruptured appendix or complicated cholecystectomy along with the fried chicken for dinner. Throughout the day think of interesting bits of conversation or anecdotes to share with the others. Conscientiously try to turn off the shop talk at 5:00 P.M. or whenever the end of the work day comes.

In a group where there are young mothers, often the whole conversation is of formulas, innoculations and teething. There certainly is a time for such discussions, but don't let that be the *sole* thing you can talk about. Little Junior is going to grow up. Then what will you do for conversation?

Don't let your mind grow stale. Be aware of what is going on outside the four walls of your house or the sphere of your work. Listen to the radio or T.V. Subscribe to news magazines to keep you up on general information and current events: *Time, Newsweek, U.S. News and World Report, Reader's Digest,* etc.—whatever appeals to you.

Keep up with what's current in the Christian world also. Subscribing to your denominational paper, *Moody Monthly, Christianity Today,* etc. will help you do this.

Continue to receive, or begin to receive the journal of whatever is your profession: medicine, nursing, teaching for example.

Subscribe to periodicals in your hobby interest: *Field and Stream, Sports Illustrated, Needle and Craft, Popular Photography, Plants Alive,* or whatever it is that gives you pleasant relaxation.

Going beyond periodicals, read good books. Have people send books to you. The home constituency often writes asking what they can send for Christmas or birthday or other special occasions. Even in countries where sending packages through the mail can create problems with the Customs Department, most often books come in duty free. Many people read paperbacks and then don't know what to do with them. Suggest that you and your friends could benefit from these. Read both Christian and secular books. Plan time into your schedule to read. Don't feel guilty as if you ought to be "doing something" when you are reading. Often the way to get your own creative idea juices stirring is to read what someone else has said about the subject. You may agree and move forward with your idea or better yet, you may disagree and come up with a whole new approach.

Now, I can hear some of you saying, "Me—find time to read! You can tell SHE doesn't have any little ones around the house! How can she talk about reading? I don't have time to read my Bible, let alone a book!"

It is a proven fact—you *do* have time to do what you want to do. For a while during my first year in Chittagong, I lived in an apartment above the Walsh family. Jay Walsh was engrossed in a pioneer ministry to a group of tribal people, and his wife Eleanor, a nurse, was very busy with their seven children. The oldest child was ten when the last one was born. Yet Eleanor was probably the best read of any of us. It was important to her, so she would take time—make time is more accurate—to read. Budget reading into your time schedule.

Your own reading habits can reap dividends in the lives of your children as well. Being a good reader and being a good student are nearly always synonymous. A child who sees his parents enjoying good books will more readily pick up a book on his own, than will the child in a home where books merely adorn a shelf.

Author Joyce Landorf says, "Before I was old enough to read myself my mother instilled in me a deep love of books by reading aloud everything from Bible stories to children's classics. Ever since those days I've loved to read. I still experience the same thrill I had as a child whenever I see a new book list or finish a new book."

In *Honey for a Child's Heart,* Gladys Hunt gives a fine anthology of books suitable for children at various ages. For parents who don't know what to introduce into their children's lives, this would be a helpful book.

Guard your Emotional Well-being

This is an area that can either make or break your missionary career.

Cultivate, if you already have, or develop if you don't have, a sense of humor. It is better to laugh at yourself than to cry. Although there are times, especially for a woman, when crying is the very best thing you can do. At those times, go ahead and cry. That's a woman's privilege!

A missionary wife tells a story on herself. She and her husband had trekked in the hills all day following a long boat ride. It was the hot season and by the time they arrived back at the boat she was absolutely exhausted. Her husband found her kneeling by the stream at sundown, rubbing out clothes by hand. Tears were pouring down her cheeks. She sobbed out her woe, "I just don't think the Lord ever intended me to live like this."

Being a wise and loving man, her husband refrained from a theological discourse as to the knowledge of and problems of the Lord's will. He brought her a pillow, helped her lie down in the boat and brewed her a cup of strong tea. A short rest restored her to her good humor and she felt rather foolish, but at the moment it had been very serious.

Cry when you need to; laugh when you can. Try to develop a thick skin. Don't let everything that is said to you get you down. Proverbs 12:16, as it reads in the N.I.V. says, "A fool shows his annoyance at once, but a prudent man overlooks an insult."

The two biggest emotional problems confronting missionaries and other Christian workers are discouragement and loneliness.

Discouragement may begin before the missionary career even gets started. Setbacks during the years of preparation, financial difficulties, intensive testing, wearing deputation—these things combine to strike down all but the hardiest, all but those who have declared, "I'll get there, by God's help, no matter what!"

Then after the excitement of finally arriving on your chosen field comes the humbling time of orientation and language study. Inevitably someone catches on more quickly and it seems as though you'll never learn. This is often intensified because nationals tend to compare you with other foreigners or laugh at the way you say things.

As you get into the work, you may find yourself with that helpless feeling. You may start thinking you don't really belong here at all. Everyone else is so competent and does the work so easily and well— and then there's you! You often seem to be given things to do you don't know how to do. Someone assigns you a task and leaves you with a cheery, "Do the best you can." Or, even worse, you don't get to do the things you can do well, the things for which you gave up friends and homeland. Instead you are doing menial tasks that anybody else could accomplish. It's easy to seethe with resentment when you seem to be kept from the work you planned to do. It is easy to build up your troubles and woes until you are ready to throw in the towel and go home, Discouragement—one of Satan's strongest allies.

If you are discouraged, you do have company there. Some of God's choicest sevants, David, Elijah and the great Apostle Paul, among others, became discouraged. But they didn't stay in the Slough of Despond. You don't have to either.

Discouragements will come. They come to us all, but that is not the time for defeat, despair or running away. It is the time for practicing a quiet trust in God. Missionary Amy Carmichael wrote,

Things are sure to happen which will drain the heart of human hope, but
the hallmark of the true missionary is refusal to be weakened or harden-
ed or soured or made hopeless by disappointment.¹

Discouragement—despair—defeat—depression—all those dreadful
"D's" that can sap the strength and ruin the ministry. But those
moods usually come and go. For some people, however, the problem
which faces them is *loneliness* and it doesn't seem to go away.

Professor Craig Ellison, in *Christianity Today,* wrote:

Two basic feelings underlie loneliness. The first is a lack of the sense of
belonging. Not being chosen by others, the lonely person is unsure that
he is wanted by anyone. The second is the feeling that no one under-
stands. The lonely person has either lost or been unable to form relationships in which he can share intimate concerns with another person
who is interested, sympathetic and accepting.
    The loneliness of not feeling accepted and understood may be experi-
enced by married as well as by single people. Married persons who become too busy in separate spheres of activity, or who do not talk to each
other about deep feelings for fear of being hurt, or who fail to encourage intimate communication, are likely to experience loneliness.²

Loneliness—it can strike the missionary in various circumstances:
    I recall the thoughtful married man who lived with his family in a
remote jungle station. Across the compound lived one single lady missionary. "Sure," he said, "We invite her over to dinner, but I always
get this feeling in the pit of my stomach when I see her going back into
her house alone."
    The married couple who are the first or only missionaries in a cer-
tain area. They are completely on their own to acquaint themselves
with the field, initiate a program and provide social contacts for themselves and their children.
    The preacher husband off on a preaching tour. The missionary
word, "trekking' is a colorful descriptive word, but often it just
means long, hot hours walking in the sun over rough terrain while
blisters the size of golf balls swell on your feet. Or maybe in the urban
setting it means climbing steep stairways in squalid tenements, or
pounding the pavement on house to house visitation.
    And while he's off by himself his wife is home alone—left to cope
with servants who may resent a woman telling them what to do, and
with children who may need Dad's steadying discipline.

The missionary lady who upon arriving on her new station says, "I won't need a mailbox to myself. If I get one letter a week it's a miracle."

The missionary who doesn't hear from her family for months on end and when she is due to go home has to cable frantically to be sure they know she's coming.

During my first term I lived alone for a number of months. My roommate was home in the States first deciding to, then marrying a long time friend. During the weekdays, I was busy studying the language and teaching missionary children in a nursery school. I was often out in the evenings, but Sunday dinner was my Waterloo! I don't know why my friends and colleagues seldom invited me home after church. Week after week, I had extra salt in my diet as I cried into my solitary Sunday dinner. Perhaps it was more distressing to me because I came from a family that always rounded up strays after the service. My mother went on home to be sure the roast was cooked and my father brought home new people in the church, strangers or people who were all alone. Our family of four often doubled or tripled.

Maybe my missionary colleagues *had* issued a general invitation, "Come to our place for a meal whenever you want to." That won't do. Most people are loathe to barge in without a special invitation.

Loneliness certainly is not limited to single lady missionaries. A person who is not a missionary, living even in places where there are many outlets and opportunities, can still feel loneliness acutely. During a visit in Switzerland I shared the breakfast table with a secretary from England. Over the crunchy rolls and creamy cheese she told me she had to be careful to modulate her voice each morning when she first spoke because apart from the seven hours she sat at her desk and typed, she had no one to speak to. After not using her voice from 5 P.M. to 9 the next morning she was afraid it would come out loud and boisterous or squeaky like a bird.

While all men and women can fall prey to loneliness at certain periods of their life, there is a specific type of loneliness which attacks those in Christian service. James L. Johnson, himself a former missionary and now director of a missionary organization, calls this the "Loneliness of the life of faith." In his excellent book, *Loneliness is Not Forever,* he writes,

> The loneliness of faith comes with the realization that there really can
> be no one else, except God, who will enter into the journey. Yes, people

are there, people's faces cross the line of vision, some smile and talk politely, try to communicate interest and concern. Some do try, and some do get through. But most seem to remain a long step removed. Sympathetic, yes! But one walking by faith does not need sympathy; it is love, interest, a need for protection, even validation.

Consider missionary Hazel R., who said, "The worst part of it all is that in twenty years of mission service I never could get close enough to anyone at home to really call him a friend. People would pray for me, they said, as my name came up on the church's prayer calendar. But they could not pray for me as someone they *really knew*. Deputation is often a time of tears for me; it always has been. I desperately wanted people to accept me into their inner circles as a person, not a superhuman frontier warrior. I wanted to cry with them, laugh with them. I wanted them to do the same with me. Instead, we met, we talked, we passed each other—I did my act, they applauded, and that was that."

People who "go by faith" are often pushed out of the mainstream of human concourse by their own calling. They are set aside for "higher things," which means they can never really enter the valley again to the normal human exchange. Their act of dedication to move out under the compulsion of God ironically separates them from the concerns of those who in effect "send" them. Yet no soldier has ever gone to war without the assurance that there is a time to come home; a time to return to friends, to family, to those who love him to those who wait and eagerly anticipate touching him again and sharing all the grim and the glorious days of conflict.

As one missionary put it, "to realize that there is no fitting into the social whirls of the good life at home, never really being a part of people in the normal concourses of life, because a missionary is, after all, a breed apart—this is the crushing load of the cross to me, what Jesus surely must have felt many times, what everybody must feel who puts the hand to the plow. No one thinks of these things at the time of calling or commitment, because we feel it is something God will take care of Himself, and He does—in the end, He does. But these pressures can still bring those moments, those days, of loneliness, and in those times you feel fragile as a human being and even as a servant of God."[3]

Maybe missionaries themselves are at fault for perpetuating the "superman" image in their prayer letters and reports to home constituencies. If we missionaries aren't willing to share our mistakes, our problems, our frustrations with other people, of course they will assume we are above these common trials of life. Then it is we ourselves who suffer. This is the case whether we are at home or on the mission field. We lose ordinary contact with other "Christian workers" who happen to work in the hometown post office or teach in the local pub-

lic school rather than living and working half way around the world.
Maybe by being more open with our supporters, we would get rid of
the ideas expressed by a lady who told me, "I'd like to correspond
with you, but I live such an ordinary life. I don't know what I'd write
to a missionary.

Bless your heart, lady. I'm just as interested in the price of coffee
these days, and what Mrs. So and So wore to the church wedding as
you are. And I *need* you to tell me things—common, everyday things,
just to keep me in touch with life.

Perhaps we have not conveyed that need clearly enough to people
back in the homelands. They don't know how much we need their fellowship in prayer and by the spoken and the written word. We leave
sign-up sheets on the table at the rear of the church for those who wish
to receive our prayer letters. Many people sign up. For reasons of
economy we trim the list down by asking those who are really interested to fill in a card and mail it to an address in the United States.
Still the response is up in the hundreds. But then we don't hear from
those people ever—until the next round of deputation when we start
all over with the sign-up sheet.

Oh, there are exceptions: the little child who says, "I have your pic-
ture over my bed. I pray for you every night before I go to sleep." Or
the new widow who says, "Jeannie, you've lost a prayer warrior. My
husband prayed for you down on his knees everyday of his life."
Those expressions of love and concern are humbling.

But what becomes of all the rest who are names on the prayer letter
list but you don't know if they are alive or dead? What of the churches
who regularly send in their money, but you never know if they have a
different pastor, new program or have even moved to a new location.

One of my biggest disappointments in the line of not hearing from
those I expected to hear from came during one of the biggest blessings
of my missionary career. For over ten years our fledgling Literature
Division occupied rooms in rented buildings. Three times we outgrew
these until in the last house, there were books stored under the beds
and wedged in every possible space. We had to get our meals over
quickly because two secretaries worked at our dining room table. And
then God started working miracles. Money was provided to enable us
to look for property of our own; we located and were finally able to
obtain clear title to a choice piece of land; an elderly couple came to
supervise the construction of our two-story Bible Literature Centre.
That too is all another story. When the time came for the service of dedication, I sent invitations to those who were closest to me and to

those who had shown interest as I kept then informed of develop-
ments. We allowed time in the program for the reading of messages
which had come by letter and telegram. There was a good representa-
tion, some from surprising sources, but what disappointed me was
those who not then, nor since have thought to write and thank God
with us. For years I had lived, breathed, slept the possibility of a literature production center. This was the fulfillment of that dream and
some churches and friends never even mentioned it.

Conversely, one of my greatest blessings in the years of service overseas has been regular letters from my family. Lengthy accounts of
happenings, newsclippings, jokes, cards—things that say, "You're being thought of." In addition to his regular letters, my brother Bruce
has made it his practice that whenever business or pleasure takes him
to a particular building in New York, my favorite city, he always sends
me a note on their stationery. It takes time out of his schedule, but I
appreciate it.

Loneliness can strike from many sources, both while on the mission
field and when at home. The question comes then: What to do when
loneliness, depression, despair set in.

First *recognize what you are dealing with.* Again quoting from
Johnson's book on *Loneliness:*

> "Many people cannot distinguish between loneliness, aloneness and
> solitude, confusing them all as being detrimental to the human spirit.
> Solitude, however, is an aloneness that is, or can be creative. Solitude
> brings self-discovery. It allows the mind to untangle itself. Solitude is to
> let the mind and emotions drain away, free from the demands of others.
> Solitude is not loneliness and need not be a crippler. It need not lead to
> despair. The secret of having times of solitude is in understanding that
> this is not a process for ill but an opportunity for God to show Himself
> as perhaps He cannot do when the landscape becomes too crowded."[4]

Consider the possible causes:

If you find yourself unexplainably tired, weepy, losing interest in
your work and life around you, check with your doctor. It may be that
your emotional depression has a treatable physical cause. One Christian doctor said, "I learned long ago that if a person can no longer
pray, the problem might be as simple as a thyroid deficiency." Don't
berate yourself needlessly. Go to your doctor, then follow his prescription whether it is for multivitamins, or a daily siesta, or a month's
vacation.

Having consulted with your doctor, it might be wise to check your

Spiritual signs and symptoms. Apathy, dullness, wanting to "throw in the towel," overwhelming loneliness—any of these symptoms can be masking a broken relationship with the Lord. Perhaps there is an area of your life which you have been unwilling to turn over to the Lord; perhaps you are harboring bitterness toward or fostering a critical spirit among your fellow workers. Thank God for the convicting power of the Holy Spirit working in your life to bring these things to light. Claim the promise of forgiveness in I John 1:9. Confess the problem and allow the Great Physician to work in your life.

The Therapy of Work:

When loneliness or discouragement come, don't give in to them, rather *work them off*. One of the best antidotes for depression is a demanding job. If emotional problems are threatening, tackle some housecleaning, get out and work in the garden, engage in vigorous physical exercise, but do something. George Bernard Shaw wrote.

"The surest way to be miserable is to have the leisure to wonder whether or not you are happy."

Perhaps more than any other time, when a woman is feeling lonely she needs to guard against the sin of self pity. "Poor little me! Here I am all alone. Nobody's ever had it as bad as I have." What a waste of time just to sit and feel sorry for yourself. Get up and do something! Do something you enjoy. Cook up a fancy dish. Cut out a pattern. Work on your needlepoint. Again referring to the Walsh family, we, upstairs could always tell when Jay was away and Eleanor was feeling lonely. She would get out the most difficult piano pieces. We could hear her rattling those keys for all she was worth. That was her way of working off a slump. Find your own method, but do something.

If your problems are too heavy for you, *tell somebody about them.* Don't bottle it all up. Tell the Lord, of course, but also tell someone else. Perhaps some new arrangements can be worked out. Maybe you can move to a new location. Maybe two families can move closer together. Or a short term worker can come to live with you for a while. Maybe members of your own family can come for a visit. All my immediate family have managed to do this. With today's easier air travel and excursion fares, having someone come to stay with you is a valid option. Remember, people are more important than work, however important the work may be. If you're lonely or discouraged ask for help. It is quite likely something can be done to help you.

Of course, in the final analysis, the solution to the problems of loneliness, of discouragement or of any of the other destructive emotions which drain the soul and weaken the body, is a total trust in a loving Heavenly Father.

Finally from *Loneliness is not Forever,*

> Taking all the human props away then (if that be the case), the man or woman living a life of faith, trusting the light he or she has for the journey commissioned by God, is still never alone. That has become too familiar, of course, but the truth still does not wear out with the using. The mystery of the presence of God in such a life has kept thousands of Christians in the bleakest, darkest, most solitary situations on earth. That is why prison cells do not bend them; the heat and sun of the jungles and deserts do not crack them; wind, fire, and cold do not subdue them; the endless, empty prairies or the crowded metropolises of indifferent masses have not deterred them; in it all, the man or woman of God knows the "presence" and the "still, small voice."
>
> For the one who holds God close and knows what that "still small voice" means in the dark hours, there is that promise, "Lo, I am *with you always,* even to the end of the age" (Matthew 28:20).⁵

By whatever means, by *all* means, taking care of ourselves is the practical way to "present our bodies a living sacrifice", and effectively continue in the ministry to which we have been called.

[1]Amy Carmichael, *Gold Cord* (Fort Washington, Christian Literature Crusade, 1957), page 75.

[2]Craig Ellison, "The Roots of Bitterness", Copyright by *Christianity Today,* March 10, 1978, used by permission.

[3]James L. Johnson, *Loneliness Is Not Forever* (Chicago: Moody Press, 1979), pages 90-92.

[4]*Ibid,* excerpts from pages 177 to 187.

[5]*Ibid.*

Chapter Eight

The Challenge of Peaceful Living

In his injunction that we live peaceably with all men, (Romans 12:18) even the Apostle Paul must have known how hard a struggle this can be. (I trust he was using the generic term "men"; not implying that it is NOT possible for women to live to live at peace with one another.) In his book, *Facing the Field,* Dr. Soltau counsels

"It often happens that two or more families or individuals are thrown together in the same mission station who, from the standpoint of temperament or culture, seem to have very little in common. Had they lived in the same town at home, they would, in all probability, never have formed a friendship that was in any sense close. On the mission field, however, they may easily be the only Westerners in the city and are entirely dependent upon each other for their spiritual and social life. Grace will often be required to keep relations between them sweet, but the giver of all grace is able to grant it in sufficient quantity so as to insure victory.

On the other hand when two or more families or individuals are compatible, the combined impact of their work and influence is cumulative. The moral and spiritual discipline which they undergo as they work together, checking and counterchecking on each other's efforts, precludes the tendency toward becoming dictatorial and 'difficult'. In the long run they will accomplish much more, both quantitatively and qualitatively, than had they been placed singly and alone in different places."[1]

Distance, isolation, loneliness, pressure of surrounding heathenism, the necessities of the common work: these all unite to force missionaries into closer circumstances than is true of Christian workers elsewhere. In such circumstances small annoyances which under other conditions might go unnoticed, are apt to be magnified and develop into serious irritations.

A missionary doctor said of an ongoing conflict, "If I have to build them with my own hands, I am going to get each of these single women into a house of her own. Their constant squabbling is driving us all crazy." If justified, what a terrible indictment!

Learn to live peaceably.

As an *unmarried person* you may be delegated to live with someone you would not have chosen to have a cup of coffee or a coke with at home. You have nothing in common with this person. Maybe she is old enough to be your mother. Or, in this era when age limits are not the serious barrier to missionary service, you as a mature person with one career already behind you, might arrive for missionary service to find your "senior missionary" barely more than a giggling teenager—at least in your eyes. Still the decree comes: "Live peaceably." God knew it would not be easy. He knew it would be a learning process.

Women living in the same house need time to work out their day-by-day arrangements. It takes as much time and effort learning to adjust to the living situation when you are not married, as it does when you are. In fact one widowed lady, serving in a short-term missionary capacity remarked, "I didn't have half the trouble cooking for my husband that I do for the girls in my house."

A harmonious living situation doesn't just happen. It has to be worked at. It takes trial and error. Here are three proven suggestions:

Very early as you are organizing your household structure, set aside a time to pray together.

Keep short accounts with one another.

Get a touchy matter straightened out just as soon as possible.

I am grateful for the first roommates I had as a new missionary. One was a dear friend with whom I had traveled on deputation and out to the field. She and I moved in with a girl who had arrived a few years before us and therefore was our senior missionary. She often regimented us, bossed us about (all for our ultimate welfare as we admitted later on). But sometimes I rebelled at her telling me what to do. I remember one stormy breakfast when we were at loggerheads. She left to tutor a language class of new missionaries, and I stayed to babysit all their kids. She had been gone barely a few minutes when she returned. "I couldn't leave it like that," she said. A reconciliation, a brief prayer—and we were both freed to enjoy the day before us. Don't harbor resentments. Don't allow bitterness to grow up between you and those with whom you live.

And here are some other don'ts to consider:

Be careful that in your honest search for harmony in the home you don't lose your identity. Don't bury yourself in your housemate's life. You don't have to live in each other's pocket. Be a person in your own right.

Don't be a leech, always clinging to your roommate or to one particular girl. Circumstances change so fast. Enjoy the situation you are in but allow for the possibility of a change in location, job or marital status in the future.

If you have a roommate, be sure to get across to her and to the rest of your associates that you two are not Siamese twins. You don't have to do everything together. You don't have to be invited out together. You don't have to take vacations together. It's better if the two of you do have separate interests which you then can talk about when you are together. Learn to say No to an invitation if you don't feel like going, but do this with sensitivity. Your No may deprive your roommate who does wish to go.

Be considerate of a more gregarious, outgoing type of person, but don't dedicate yourself to being her social secretary. Strive to be thoughtful, helpful and kind, while still maintaining your own personality and interests.

A word of caution, even as we are talking about creating an attitude of kindness and concern. Some beautiful friendships have developed between ladies who have lived and worked and suffered and cried together. But especially in this day of loose morals, be careful that the relationship does not develop along physical lines. As St. Augustine described it so long ago. "Some pollute the stream of friendship with the sludge of unbridled sex." Satan would love to take what could be a fine, wholesome relationship and corrupt it into homosexual depravity.

In the area of daily living, *married couples* have the advantage. They have chosen each other rather than having been placed with a housemate. They already know each other's shortcomings and faults—at least those which surface in a relatively stable environment and temperate climate. They have love to buffer the bad spots in life. But even in the best of marriages, new problems will develop with the stresses of a new culture, new responsibilities, even different food and weather conditions.

Married couples need to plan dates, times when they can be alone together. A word to the unmarried: don't feel bad if a couple go off by themselves. Don't always want to be a tag-along. Don't always have to be part of every group. Let them enjoy themselves; you could offer to babysit so that they can have a time away from the pressures of the family.

As was suggested for the singles living in close quarters, the married folks, too, need to keep short accounts with one another and with God. Don't let resentments build up until they are irreconcilable.

Sometimes just the differences in personality—that which makes a person uniquely what he or she is—can be the very thing that causes friction. One person might be very sociable, always wanting to have company in, always wanting to be on the go. The other one might be shy and reserved, a homebody who would much rather stay in. One might be a perfectionist, a stickler for neatness in the home; the other one might like the house to have that lived-in look.

Whether in the case of roommates or marriage partners, recognize the basic differences in temperament. If you have never read Tim La-Haye's *Spirit Controlled Temperament,* or it has been a while since you read it, you will do well to go through it again. While you may not subscribe to that particular line of psychology, it will help you to understand that generally people act the way they do because they were made that way, not because they are deliberately trying to annoy you!

When Lynn and I first started sharing a home, I often distressed her unwittingly. Coming in from a lesson or a medical call, I would drop whatever I had been using on the nearest table and let them lie there until I had time for a grand slam clean up. Lynn, on the other hand, wanted them put where they belonged right away, working on the very proper assumption that perhaps the great clean up might not materialize for a while. I certainly didn't mean to annoy her: leaving the things out in plain sight was an incentive to me to get that needed tidy-up job. Looking back I could see that I had always been one to do things in a big way. During those Saturday morning clean ups in my parsonage home, many times I would pull everything out of the drawers and cupboards to be resorted and organized rather than running the vacuum cleaner or routinely dusting.

Traits and life-long habits are not easy to break. Be considerate with your co-workers. Each of us has quirks of personality that are irritating or offensive to others.

If the actions or characteristics of a person with whom you live or work drive you crazy, ask yourself, "Is what this person is doing adversely affecting the Lord's work, or is it just something that bothers me personally?" If the latter is the case, it could be that praying for that person will change your attitude about him entirely.

An even more penetrating question to ask yourself would be, "What am *I* doing that may be driving somebody else crazy? Are people having to spend time praying for grace to put up with me?"

A mark of maturity is to work on eliminating your own quirks and accepting those of others. Rather than deciding your colleague is out to rub salt on your wound, learn and practice the words of Jonathan Goforth of China. In 1894 he compiled seven rules for daily living. Among them, "Put the very best construction on the actions of others."

Don't ascribe underlying or ulterior motives to a person's actions. Assume he is doing what he thinks is best. God has not set you or me up as a judge over our fellow-workers.

Two quotations are applicable here. The first by Kipling, "Be slow to judge. We know little of what has been done and nothing of what has been resisted."

The other, the old American Indian adage, "Do not judge a man until you have walked a mile in his moccasins."

Be careful in handing out criticisms, whether they be of the person himself, or of his family or work. When a reprimand or a suggestion honestly does need to be given, remember the formula, "speaking the truth in love" (Ephesians 4:15a).

As much as you try to live without ruffling somebody's feathers, problems are bound to arise. The close confines within which most Christian workers live and work can be a hothouse producing friction and trouble.

What can you do when problems arise? Two words come to mind: compromise and flexibility. By definition these words mean: compromise—a settlement of differences by which each side makes concessions; flexible—responsive to change, adaptable.

These attitudes open the door for give and take on both sides. No one is ever either completely right or completely wrong; both can give a bit.

We were on a vacation in India one time—three nurses from our mission and a Peace Corps nurse. Since none of us had money for the first class hotels, we were staying overnight at mission stations along the way. (This is a perfectly acceptable arrangement with well defined guest room rates.) One evening we found ourselves in a mission house in a town in northern India. Two women lived there: one had arrived in India just after World War II and the other one, like us, had recently come to the Indian subcontinent. The older woman had carefully tutored the man who served the table that he was to bring first the

meat, then the gravy and then the potatoes. But the younger missionary liked to put the gravy on her potatoes. So she wanted meat,
potatoes, then gravy, in that order. The two were fussing over this at
every meal. They would barely speak to one another; they certainly
couldn't pray together. Our Peace Corps friend was not a believer.
This was her first introduction to missionary living. She was wide-eyed
over the gravy issue. One of us innocently suggested, "Why don't you
just put the gravy on the table? That way you could have it whenever
you want it." They hadn't thought of that solution!

There are always ways to compromise. There are always means to
be found whereby everyone can benefit.

Living peaceably is not easy. Each of us by nature is selfish. We
think our way is the only way, or at least the best way *(If everyone
would only do things our way, there would be no trouble)*. Being
human, we must consistently work at living in peace and harmony.

Dr. Donn Ketcham, in his commencement address to the High
School class of 1980 at the Malumghat Christian School, in Bangladesh, gave this "Prescription for Living Peacefully" from Colos-
sians chapter three:

   v.5—Be pure
   8,9—Be honest
    12—Be compassionate
    13—Be forgiving
    14—Be loving
    15—Be peaceful
    15—Be thankful
    16—Be thoughtful in the Word of God
    17—Be consistent so that people will know how to
        expect you will act.

Cultivating those qualities will go a long way toward creating an atmosphere of harmony among those with whom you work and live.
The importance of privacy:

Another irritant, besides differences in personality, is the failure to
observe proper respect for people's privacy.

Privacy is essentially a Western value. Especially among Americans,
there seems to be a sense of security derived from privacy. Americans
have their own bedrooms, their own closets, their own dresser
drawers, their locked diaries. They resent people peering at them, pry-
ing into their business or giving unsolicited advice.

To the Asian mind—certainly in Bangladesh—privacy is practically incomprehensible. Eastern people derive their security from together-ness. In most lower class homes, the entire family lives in one room.

If a person is ill, everyone flocks to see him and to commiserate, or to reinterpret the doctor's orders.

When a new bride goes to her husband's home her little sister goes along too so the bride won't be lonely.

Decisions are not private matters. They are made in mutual consul-tation among the older, respected members of the community then passed down to the younger ones who rarely would question or disobey. Decisions as to whom one will marry, where one will study, where one will live, what name to give to the new baby: these are all made by the group, possibly without even much consideration of the feelings of the people most closely involved. Everyone is very much his brother's keeper and will offer free advice or interfere in a situation in order to protect another person's best interests. Often a person will be swayed from heading off in a wrong direction in life, or—sadly—from accept-ing Christ as Saviour, by the expedient of reminding him of his obliga-tion to the group to which he belongs: "Who do you think you are, doing something which none of the rest of us has ever done?" And the matter is dropped there.

As part of the two worlds in which the missionary lives, he must be willing to be like a chameleon, changing his outlook as the situation demands. When nationals want to see your house—show them; when they ask questions, answer them—within reason that is! But when you return to your peer group, return privacy to its priority place on the Western value scale. This includes things such as—never, never walk into somebody's house or room without first knocking on the door or calling, "Anybody home?" or in some way announcing yourself.

Never burst in on a conversation.

Never read another person's mail, whether it's done by shuffling through his desk drawers or steaming open the envelopes. (Besides be-ing totally impolite, it could be humiliating: you might find out something about yourself you'd be happier not knowing.)

Never help yourself to somebody's clothes or car without prior per-mission. And periodically check your bookshelves to be sure you have not inadvertently become a "book-keeper."

Going deeper than respecting a person's belongings, comes the respect of the person himself. Allow people to be individuals, and families to do things differently. Your family needs some time to learn its own identity. The children need to learn, "We're the Jones's. We do it this way. At the Smith's house, they do it another way."

A few years ago, for instance, the Halloween issue came up at Malumghat where many missionary families connected with Memorial Christian Hospital live. One family felt that dressing up the missionary children as ghosts, spirits and witches could be damaging to the reputation of the family and the mission, because the local people take seriously ghosts, spirits and witches and fear them as dangerous and evil. The others thought that Halloween was just harmless fun and frivolity. Great! To each his own. Kids need to learn that they are not just part of a community of people: they belong to a family with its own separate beliefs and traditions, a heritage going back to their own previous generations.

We have been discussing the ingredients that make for peaceable relationships. One reason this is so important is the special emphasis the Lord Himself gives it:

"Blessed are the peacemakers for they shall be called the children of God." Matthew 5:9.

Every now and then we need to reflect on the question: Are human relationships smoother, more loving where I am, or do problems needlessly arise and petty contentions grow because of me?

One of our chief desires, as those people who are called to serve the Lord in what is called a full-time capacity, ought to be to create an atmosphere of harmony, love and care for one another. It ought to be that outsiders coming to our homes, our offices, our teaching areas can see the love of Christ radiating through our daily living. Only this way will our witness be credible as we endeavor to attract people to Christ. They will see Him in us, in the way we act and the way we treat our fellow workers—and will be drawn to know more about Him. Or—they will see in us bitterness, jealousies, scheming for top position, pettiness—and will turn away from Him.

I have on the door of my bedroom the famous prayer by St. Francis of Assisi. I read it often. I need to read it often. It speaks to my heart each time I read it. Perhaps it will speak to you too.

Lord, make me an instrument of Your peace.
Where there is hatred, let me show love;
Where there is injury, pardon;
Where there is doubt, faith;
Where there is despair, hope;
Where there is sadness, joy.

Our dealings with one another transcend the artificial boxes labeled Singles, Married, New Worker or Veteran. It is how we treat each other as people, as fellow members of the family of God that really counts.

[1]T. Stanley Soltau, *Facing the Fields* (Grand Rapids, Baker Book House, 1975), pages 86, 88.